ALLERGY-FREE FOOD

Recipes and practical advice to help you manage food allergies

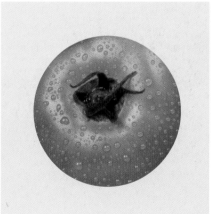
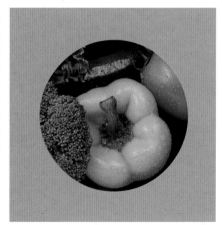

Tanya Wright

Bounty Books

ALLERGY UK is a national medical charity established to increase understanding and awareness of allergy and to help people manage their allergies. It raises funds for allergy research and provides training for health care professionals including doctors, nurses and dieticians. For further information please see www.allergyuk.org or contact us at:
Planwell House, LEFA Business Park, Edgington Way, Sidcup, Kent DA14 5BH
Tel: 01322 619898

TANYA WRIGHT is a State Registered dietician specialising in food allergy and intolerance. She has written articles for the popular press and has recently written a book about enjoying life with a food allergy. She has also worked as a consultant to the food industry and as a website dietician. Tanya is a regional coordinator for the Anaphylaxis Campaign and for the British Allergy Foundation.

First published in Great Britain in 2002 by Hamlyn
a division of Octopus Publishing Group Ltd

New hardback edition published in 2004 by Bounty Books, a division of Octopus Publishing Group Ltd
Reprinted in 2005 (twice)

This paperback edition published 2011 by Bounty Books,
a division of Octopus Publishing Group Ltd
Endeavour House
189 Shaftesbury Avenue
London WC2H 8JY

www.octopusbooks.co.uk

An Hachette UK Company
www.hachette.co.uk

Copyright © Octopus Publishing Group Ltd 2002

ISBN: 978-0-753720-53-0

A CIP catalogue record for this book is available from the British Library

Printed and bound in China

NOTES
Before embarking on an exclusion diet, seek qualified medical advice. This is especially important for children, pregnant women and nursing mothers.

Many of the recipes featured in this book use special wheat-free, gluten-free and dairy-free ingredients. These may not always give the same results as conventional cooking ingredients.

contents

Introduction

Allergy-free Food will give hope to all those who have suffered from adverse reactions or allergic responses to food, by outlining a positive plan that will lead to a diagnosis and resolution of the symptoms. Not only will this book help you identify the foods that are provoking your symptoms, it will also explain how these foods can be avoided and yet allow allergy sufferers to enjoy an interesting and varied diet that is also nutritionally complete.

By placing nutritional, social, psychological and economic stresses on sufferers and their families, food allergies and intolerances can affect the quality of life of all those who experience them. These problems are often made worse by the scepticism often expressed about food allergies and intolerances by those practising conventional medicine, and it is not unknown for sufferers to go from one practitioner to another in search of help.

The lack of reliable 'allergy tests' in mainstream medicine often leads people who suspect that they have a food allergy or intolerance but cannot get confirmation of their problem, to seek advice from practitioners of alternative medicine. This can be extremely expensive, however, and the patient may still be left without a realistic or definitive diagnosis. Faced with no other option, the patient may then resort to manipulating his or her own diet, risking poor nutrition and yet further frustration, which only compounds the whole problem.

This book enables anyone who has a food allergy or intolerance to break out of this destructive spiral and shows how eating can once again become a pleasure. The easy-to-follow advice on identifying the substance or substances at the root of the problem, and the suggestions for suitable alternatives, are followed by recipes that can be used to build up an interesting and nutritionally balanced diet that is appropriate for your particular allergy.

THE RECIPES

The recipes at the end of this book can be used both on an exclusion diet and after a food allergy or intolerance has been diagnosed. They are suitable for all the family and can be used alone or in conjunction with other recipes. Try writing out the recipes for dishes you often cook at home and code them in the same way as the recipes in this book. If you keep them all together you will have a convenient collection of recipes for the dishes you can eat. On days when you are feeling deprived of certain foods you need only look in one place to remind yourself of the foods you can still eat. The collection will also be useful for a friend or relative who wants to cook for you.

The symbols shown on the right are used so that you can see at a glance which recipes are appropriate for your circumstances and diet. There are recipes that can be used if you are following the recommended Basic Exclusion Diet or the Stricter Exclusion Diet, and these will help you to keep to these restrictive diets by offering a range of dishes that can be enjoyed by all the family. This will help you to select recipes that you can eat safely once you have identified your own particular allergy or intolerance and know which foods you need to avoid. Many of the recipes are suitable for vegetarians, and these, too, are indicated by a symbol.

Maintaining a nutritional balance on a restricted diet can be difficult, so it is important to make sure your diet provides you with the recommended daily amounts (RDAs) of nutrients, as set by the World Health Organization. Each recipe in this book shows values for energy, protein, carbohydrate, fat, fibre, calcium and iron, to help you monitor this. Shown below are the RDAs for each of these, and the main foods in which they are found.

Symbols used in this book

 cows' milk-free

 egg-free

 gluten-free

 nut-free

 wheat-free

 suitable for vegetarians

 suitable for those on a basic exclusion diet

 suitable for those on a stricter exclusion diet

	RDA	Sources
Protein	50–60 g (2–2¼ oz)	Meat, fish, eggs, milk, nuts, pulses
Carbohydrate	250–300 g (8–10 oz)	Refined sources, e.g. sugar, confectionery Unrefined sources, e.g. potatoes, rice, pasta, bread, cereals
Fat	70–90 g (2¾–3½ oz)	Oil, butter, fat on meat, dairy products, pastry, fried food
Fibre	30 g (1¼ oz)	Vegetables, fruit, wholegrain cereals, pulses
Calcium	700 mg	Milk and dairy products, canned fish (including bones), nuts, seeds, cereals
Iron	9 mg	Red meat, eggs, cereals, treacle, curry powder, pulses

Energy	Female: approx 2000 kilocalories (8400 kilojoules) Male: approx 2500 kilocalories (10,500 kilojoules)

What are food allergies & intolerances?

Common allergy-provoking foods include strawberries, cheese and tomatoes.

The expression 'food allergy' is widely used to mean any unpleasant reaction to a food that results in one or more physical symptoms. Strictly speaking, the word 'allergy' applies to responses made by the body's immune system; other adverse reactions to foods should be called 'food intolerances'. In both cases, if the problem food is avoided the symptoms should disappear.

FOOD ALLERGY

True food allergy is more common in children than in adults. Many children will grow out of a food allergy, just as many grow out of eczema, and a steep fall in allergic response generally occurs between the ages of three and five.

Certain people (known as atopic) produce excessive amounts of an antibody called IgE (immunoglobulin E) in response to some foods, pollens or animal fur. The high levels of IgE cause immediate reactions, such as urticaria and anaphylaxis, within minutes of eating an offending food. Atopic people are also prone to delayed reactions to foods, when symptoms such as eczema, asthma or migraine may not appear for several hours or even days.

FOOD INTOLERANCE

Food intolerance can occur in a number of ways. Certain substances – namely caffeine in tea, coffee and cola drinks; tyramine in cheese, yeast and red wine; and histamine in beer, cheese, chocolate and canned fish – can provoke a wide range of symptoms, including migraine, flushing, diarrhoea and vomiting. Other foods, notably tomatoes and strawberries, cause the body to release histamine into the bloodstream, which in turn causes symptoms ranging from flushing to a drop in blood pressure. Susceptibility to these naturally occurring chemicals differs from one individual to another.

FOOD AVERSION

An adverse reaction to a food may have a psychological, rather than physical cause, such as when someone associates sickness with a particular food. If morning sickness has caused a woman to vomit after eating a certain food, for example, she may feel sick at the mention or smell of it. The cause of such an aversion may be self-evident, or may require the patient to undertake allergy or intolerance tests, exclusion diets and food challenges. In a food challenge the patient is given tastes of a number of dishes, with and without the suspect food, which should not be identifiable by sight or taste. This test should be done in a hospital under carefully controlled conditions.

Conditions caused by allergy & intolerance

SKIN

Eczema

This distressing and persistent condition, which is also known as atopic dermatitis, can develop at any age, but is particularly common in pre-school children. Many children outgrow eczema, however, and there is often a significant improvement by the age of five.

Typically, an itchy red rash appears, most often on the face and on the skin behind the knees and inside the elbows, but in severe cases the whole body may be affected. The skin becomes thickened and cracked, often weeping and bleeding. It is extremely itchy and can affect the sufferer's sleep, concentration and confidence.

Research has shown that eczema is often associated with foods such as cows' milk, eggs, fish and nuts, although it can be triggered by any food. Identifying the offending food is not as easy as in urticaria (see below), because food-induced eczema does not usually become apparent until several hours, sometimes days, after the offending food has been eaten. Carefully planned dietary measures are therefore needed to identify and eliminate the food that is causing the problem. Eczema sufferers and especially parents of children with eczema should ensure that they have minimized other common triggers, such as house dust mites and pet fur, before experimenting with various dietary exclusions. Although many cases respond favourably to dietary measures, strict medical supervision should be sought so that the diet is not depleted of nutrients. The relief obtained from the new diet may be anything from a total elimination of the eczema to a mild improvement. In some cases the benefits from dietary measures will be too small to merit the avoidance of certain foods.

Urticaria

This common condition, also known as hives, is seen in all age groups, but is particularly troublesome in children. It can begin at any age but occurs most often between weaning and the age of two, after which it often disappears.

White, fluid-filled lumps appear on the skin following direct contact with an offending substance, and, if it is a food, the lips and face will be affected. Urticarial reactions usually occur within seconds or minutes of eating or coming into contact with the food. Factors such as exercise, warmth and anxiety can lower the threshold at which food-induced urticaria occurs.

Children are more likely to suffer from food allergies than adults, but many children outgrow them by the time they reach school age.

People who develop urticaria should recall all the foods they have eaten during the hour or two before the reaction appears, so that offending foods can be identified and eliminated from the diet.

RESPIRATORY DISORDERS

Asthma

Asthma is now an extremely common disorder among children and adults. According to the World Health Organization, the incidence of asthma in Western Europe has doubled since 1990 and has increased by over 60 per cent in the United States since the early 1980s. Environmental factors such as poor ventilation in buildings and the more widespread use of wall-to-wall carpeting and soft furnishings, are a significant factor in the increasing prevalence of asthma.

The condition is characterized by coughing, wheezing and difficulty in breathing. Asthmatic attacks are usually triggered by dust, animal fur and feathers, house dust mites and pollen, but food can also be implicated. There have been many reports of dramatic improvements in some people who undertake dietary measures, and it appears that minuscule amounts of some foods can trigger a reaction. Onset time can be delayed but is more likely to be immediate. A restricted diet should be recommended only if it brings a marked improvement in the condition, particularly when the sufferer is a child.

Rhinitis

The symptoms of this condition are a runny, snuffly nose; there may also be sneezing and itchy eyes. Hay fever, which is known as seasonal rhinitis, is one form and generally occurs in the spring and summer months. The other form, perennial rhinitis, may be exacerbated by factors such as feathers, animal fur and house dust mites. It may also be associated with a food allergy, and following a diagnostic diet may help to identify whether it is food related. As with asthma, onset time can be delayed but is more likely to be immediate.

BOWEL DISORDERS

Coeliac disease

This disorder, also known as gluten enteropathy, has been unequivocally identified as being related to diet. Gluten, a protein present in wheat, rye, barley and oats (see page 30), damages the lining of the small bowel and prevents the proper digestion and absorption of nutrients. This leads to weight loss, diarrhoea and vitamin deficiencies. Even small amounts of gluten can cause problems, and gluten is found in many foods.

Asthma is sometimes related to food allergy and changes in diet can alleviate the symptoms.

Diagnosis and treatment by a specialist, and expert advice from a dietician are essential. People suffering from coeliac disease should use only those recipes that are specifically coded as suitable for a gluten-free diet. Wheat-free recipes should not be chosen because they may include other gluten-containing cereals. Fortunately, once a gluten-free diet is followed, the symptoms of coeliac disease disappear completely.

Cows' milk protein allergy

This allergy, which is also known as cows' milk protein intolerance or cows' milk-sensitive enteropathy, mainly affects babies in the first year of life – more usually those who have been bottle-fed. Symptoms, which often start after an episode of gastroenteritis, include vomiting, diarrhoea, colic and poor weight gain. Fortunately, most babies grow out of the condition.

Inflammatory bowel disease

The term inflammatory bowel disease is used for two separate conditions, both of which mainly affect young adults: ulcerative colitis and Crohn's disease. Ulcerative colitis, a disease of the large bowel, is characterized by bloody diarrhoea and, in more severe cases, anaemia, general weakness and weight loss. Crohn's disease, which affects the small intestine, is characterized by more variable symptoms, including stomach ache, diarrhoea and weight loss.

Dietary modifications have been found to ease both problems in some cases, but they should be undertaken only with the help of a dietician because of the risks of malnutrition associated with these conditions.

Irritable bowel syndrome (IBS)

This is a common syndrome, but it is often difficult to diagnose. The usual symptoms are severe, cramp-like stomach ache with diarrhoea, or sometimes alternating episodes of constipation and diarrhoea. Although there are no agreed causes for the condition, dietary changes have been found to be helpful in the reduction of the debilitating symptoms in many cases.

Lactose intolerance

Lactose is a sugar that occurs naturally in milk. Lactase, the enzyme needed to digest lactose, is present at birth but sometimes disappears after babyhood. For genetic reasons, it is particularly common in people of African and Caribbean descent. The symptoms are a bloated stomach and diarrhoea, which occur soon after drinking milk. Some people can tolerate up to a glass of milk with no adverse effects, whereas others cannot tolerate even tiny amounts. Following a lactose-free diet for a limited period can help in the diagnosis of this condition, which can then be confirmed by a doctor.

Oats.

Wheat flakes.

Rye flakes.

Pot barley.

OTHER CONDITIONS

Food allergy has been implicated in a number of other illnesses, although further research is needed to confirm the connection.

Anaphylaxis

This is the most extreme form of food allergy. It affects the whole body, usually within minutes of exposure to the allergen. The symptoms include swelling of the throat and mouth, difficulty in breathing, itchy hives (urticaria) all over the body and collapse. Without an emergency injection of adrenaline this condition can be fatal. Under no circumstances should anyone with this condition attempt any type of dietary manipulation without consulting a doctor.

Attention deficit disorder with hyperactivity (ADDH)

The possibility that hyperactive behaviour in children is related to foods or additives has been debated since the 1920s, and it is an immensely controversial topic. Dietary management is justified if it improves the quality of lives of children and their families without imposing any psychological, nutritional or economic stresses on any family member.

Autism

Casein and gluten intolerance have been associated with autism in recent years, but the connection is shrouded in controversy. It is essential to seek the advice of a dietician for more information to determine if it is appropriate to attempt dietary manipulation.

Migraine

Migraine is usually referred to as episodes of recurrent headaches, which vary in intensity, frequency and duration. They are often accompanied by nausea and vomiting, and sufferers complain that bright lights hurt their eyes. Food as a sole cause of migraine is uncommon, but many patients experience significant relief if they change their diets. Milk, cheese, chocolate, fish, wine and coffee are commonly associated with bouts of migraine.

Multiple sclerosis, rheumatoid arthritis and schizophrenia

Among the many conditions that have at various times been linked to food allergies or intolerances are multiple sclerosis, rheumatoid arthritis and schizophrenia. None of these links have been established beyond doubt, however, although there is much anecdotal evidence to support the view that a change in diet might help with these diseases. Specialist advice should be sought for all these complaints.

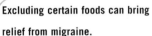

Excluding certain foods can bring relief from migraine.

Diagnosing food allergies & intolerances

At present, the only reliable way of detecting a food allergy is to remove all potentially allergy- or intolerance-provoking foods from the diet and reintroduce them one by one, to identify the food, or foods, that brings on or exacerbates a condition. This is the basis of an exclusion diet.

LABORATORY TESTS

Laboratory tests for allergies have a limited use in detecting food allergy as they give a correct diagnosis in only 60–70 per cent of cases, and sometimes they can lead to incorrect diagnosis by giving a false result. When they are used in combination with a full investigation into the patient's medical history, however, they can be of use. The reliability of laboratory tests for food intolerance is questionable.

There are two main types of medical diagnostic testing for true food allergy, *in vivo* and *in vitro* tests, and both types will be carried out by your own doctor or by a specialist in a hospital. *In vivo* tests, which evaluate the body's response to the controlled administration of particular allergens, include skin-prick testing and patch tests. Skin-prick testing is carried out by gently pricking a food extract into the skin and noting any reaction, which usually takes the form of an urticarial rash or swelling. The test is quick and painless and relatively inexpensive.

In vitro tests, which look for the presence of IgE antibodies to specific food allergens in a blood sample, include the radioallergosorbent test (RAST) and enzyme-linked immunosorbent assay (ELISA). The blood tests give much the same information as skin-prick tests, but they are more time consuming and expensive to carry out and the results are not immediate.

Other tests, such as the pulse test and the sublingual test, have not stood up well to scientific study and cannot be recommended.

UNORTHODOX TESTS

Unorthodox forms of testing, such as hair analysis, sweat tests and radionics, have no scientific basis and can be dangerous for the following reasons:

- Incorrect diagnosis.
- Failure to recognize and treat a genuine disease.
- Medically unqualified staff.
- Lack of an adequate review procedure for patients who are excluding foods from their diets.
- Inappropriate dietary advice.

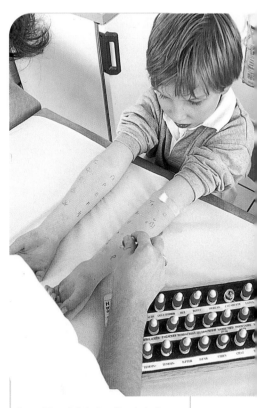

In a skin-prick test, a tiny hole is punctured in the skin and a small amount of an allergen is dropped on to it. If the patient is allergic to a substance, the skin will turn red and swell up.

Diagnostic diets

Stage 1

Keep a food diary (see page 14). By keeping a careful note of what you eat and when your symptoms occur, you may be able to pinpoint foods to avoid.

Stage 2

If you cannot identify the problem food or foods from a food diary, you will need to exclude a wide range of foods from your diet, by following a basic exclusion diet (see pages 17–19). Continue to keep a detailed diary so that the results can be compared. By the end of this stage, you should either be symptom free or greatly improved. If there is no improvement, adopt a stricter diet or revert to your usual diet.

Stage 3

Reintroduce excluded foods into your diet one by one. If your problem is diet related this will enable you to identify which foods are causing your symptoms.

Stage 4

You can now plan a nutritionally satisfactory diet, excluding the problem food.

Of course, if you already know that you cannot tolerate certain foods – shellfish or strawberries, for example – you will be able to avoid them without too much trouble. However, if you suspect that you may be allergic to, or intolerant of, a particular food or foods, but are not sure which ones trigger your symptoms, adopting a plan may help to reveal the food that causes the problem. Any plan that aims to identify such foods is called a diagnostic diet. There are four main stages to a diagnostic diet (see left).

If your problem is caused by an allergy to something you eat, the diagnostic diet will help you to identify the problem ingredient so that you can plan a nutritionally complete and appetizing diet that avoids the foods to which you are allergic or intolerant.

Planning a diagnostic diet

When you are following an exclusion diet you need to avoid certain foods for a period of three weeks. If your symptoms improve, you can begin the reintroduction phase, during which you reintroduce a food every two or three days. If you have an adverse reaction to one of these foods, allow the symptoms to clear before you attempt to reintroduce anything else. Remember to keep a detailed food and symptom diary throughout the process.

Do not undertake an exclusion diet before you have thought through the implications of being on the diet. Do not start when you have a holiday or special social function looming, and before you begin, make sure that you have a cupboard well stocked with all the permitted foods. It is also important that you give yourself plenty of time to fill in the food diary completely every time you eat or drink something, and choose a period when you will have extra time to spend in the kitchen to make the recipes from the 'allowed' foods list.

Make life easier for yourself by making some of the appropriate dishes in the recipe section (see pages 39–125) to put in the freezer. Plan the meals for the three weeks you will be on a diet, because if you have prepared meals in advance you will not be so likely to abandon your diet if your schedule alters suddenly or if there is an unforeseen emergency at home.

Some people find it helpful to contact others who have been on a restricted diet and to get tips from them on problems they may not have anticipated. Your dietician or allergy support group may be able to help with this, and there are a number of allergy sites with chat rooms on the Internet.

The greatest problems you will encounter will be with manufactured foods, which may have unclear or incomplete labels. You will need to obtain lists of food derivatives to avoid — for example, if you are avoiding milk you must also avoid, among other ingredients, casein, whey and lactose, and if you are avoiding eggs you must also avoid egg lecithin, albumin and other ingredients derived from eggs. Some of these alternative names are listed on pages 26–34, but remember that most manufactured foods contain preservatives and additives, which should be avoided while you are following an exclusion diet.

Embarking on a diagnostic diet

Before you undertake a diagnostic diet, you should consider the following health-related factors:

- The severity of your symptoms; if they are mild, it may be preferable not to follow a restricted diet at all.
- Your general health and any existing medical conditions.
- Any prescribed medication you are taking.
- Your nutritional status. For example, if you play a lot of sport, or if you are pregnant or lactating, you may have specific nutritional requirements.
- Whether you have tried an exclusion diet before.
- Whether you are already following a restricted diet — for cultural or ethical reasons, for example.
- Any existing allergies or intolerances.

As long as your reaction is not a severe one, you can test problem foods by reintroducing them, perhaps twice a year, to see whether your tolerance has changed. Some people find that they tolerate an increasing amount of a food over time, while others can tolerate a food only in its cooked form. For a minority of people dietary restrictions may be life-long.

Family and friends

Make sure that everyone in your family understands why you are embarking on your diet. If they know what you are trying to achieve, they will be more supportive and helpful. You should also make sure that colleagues at work and your friends know that you are on a special diet so that they do not tempt you to break it by offering unsuitable snacks.

Diet checklist

The success of a diagnostic diet will depend on the following factors:

- The taste and acceptability of the food ingredients.
- The cost of the food ingredients.
- Adequate facilities for cooking and eating when you are away from home.
- Making follow-up plans and ensuring you have the support and time to carry them out.
- The timing of your diet: making sure it does not coincide with holiday plans, celebrations or other social commitments.
- A selection of treats to help you to stick to the diet.
- Family support and encouragement.

Keeping a food diary

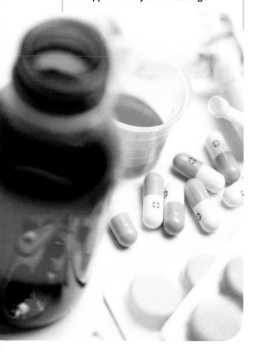

It is important to make a note in your food diary of any medication or supplements you are taking.

Keeping a diary should enable you to identify problem food or foods and to see any patterns that emerge in your response to various foods.

The object of a food diary is to identify possible links between your food and drink and the symptoms that develop. The diary must be as detailed and as accurate as possible. It is important to note both the time you eat something and the time when any symptoms develop, as you may begin to observe a pattern. You should also make a note of the severity of your symptoms, which may help you identify which food is causing the reaction. See the table below for an example of how to organize your diary.

As well as making a note of all your food and drinks, you should write down details of anything else you take orally, including medicines, nutritional supplements and even mouthwash. Keep the labels of any manufactured foods for reference. If possible, fill in the diary whenever you eat something, rather than waiting until the end of the day, so that you do not forget any small snacks or drinks.

Keep your diary for a month and check your notes. If you are allergic to a few foods and eat them rarely, the offending items should quickly become apparent. Depending on the condition, the length of time between eating the food and the onset of symptoms will vary from a matter of minutes to several days. The longer the delay, the more difficult it will be to pinpoint the culprit food or foods. The length of time that your reactions continue will also vary.

The ease with which you are able to identify these foods will determine the type of exclusion diet that you should now undertake.

Date	Time	Food/drink consumed	Symptoms	Time	Scale*

* Symptoms should be graded on a scale of 1 to 4: 1 = mild,
2 = mild to moderate, 3 = moderate, 4 = severe

Coping with nutritional problems

Following an exclusion diet is not easy, and it is important to monitor your general health and to make sure that you have an adequate supply of vitamins and minerals in your diet.

WEIGHT

Eating enough energy-rich foods is often a problem for someone who is following an exclusion diet. Many people experience weight loss, largely owing to water and body fat losses, at the start of the diet. It is important to bear in mind that exclusion diets are not designed to be slimming diets. If maintaining your weight is a problem, therefore, eat as much of the 'allowed foods' as you like.

Always eat three meals a day, and top up with some of the snacks that are suitable for your particular diet from the baking section on pages 90–113. The energy value of each recipe is indicated, so you can easily estimate your daily energy intake from the recipes. If you are overweight when you start the diet or if you begin to gain too much weight as you follow the diet, select recipes with a lower energy value. Avoid sugary foods and items such as biscuits and cakes, which contain a lot of hidden fat. Try not to fry food or use too much butter or margarine.

CONSTIPATION

When you follow a restricted diet that is low in dietary fibre, constipation can be a problem. The fibrous part of cereals, vegetables and fruit bulks out the stool, and if your diet excludes one or more of these major food sources, you may suffer from constipation. Make sure that you drink at least 2 litres (3½ pints) of fluid every day and choose plenty of fruit, vegetables and cereals from the allowed list on your chosen diet.

VITAMIN AND MINERAL DEFICIENCY

To make sure that your intake of vitamins and minerals is adequate while you are on a restricted diet it is a good idea to take a multi-vitamin and multi-mineral preparation as a supplement. These are widely available. If you are uncertain about which one is appropriate for you, ask your doctor for advice. Aim for a preparation that offers 100 per cent of the recommended daily amount (RDA) for every vitamin and mineral and check the nutritional information on the label. It is possible to take too much of some vitamins and minerals, so if you are concerned about overdoses, seek professional advice.

Reasons for failure

There are several reasons why people find it difficult to keep to an exclusion diet, and being aware of the factors before you embark on the diet may make it easier for you to keep to your plans. The factors include:

- A poor understanding of how the diet works.
- Bland, tasteless food.
- Lack of support from friends and family.
- Unrealistic expectations of the outcome of the diet.
- Unrealistic dietary constraints that impose too many limits on your lifestyle.

Is an exclusion diet suitable for you?

Exclusion diets

Adopting an exclusion diet is a reliable method of finding out if your symptoms are caused by an allergy to or intolerance of a particular food. The following foods are among those that are most frequently associated with provoking an adverse reaction:

- Alcohol
- Berry fruits
- Chocolate
- Citrus fruits
- Coffee
- Colourings
- Cows' milk
- Eggs
- Fish
- Nuts
- Preservatives
- Tomatoes
- Wheat

Before you embark on the basic exclusion diet, or the stricter version, you should check with your doctor that dietary measures are suitable for you, particularly if you have additional health complaints that are unrelated to food intolerance. It may be safe for you to undertake the diet alone, or you may require the supervision of a dietician.

If you are taking any medication, it may be possible to stop this during the food-testing period. Many medicines contain colourings, preservatives and fillers, including lactose and wheat starch, to which you may be allergic. There are alternatives for many medicines, which are usually in a syrup form. Never stop taking a prescribed medication without consulting a doctor.

COELIAC DISEASE

If you suffer from this, you should not follow an exclusion diet. Your doctor or dietician will prescribe a special diet and you will be able to use the gluten-free recipes in this book. Remember that wheat-free recipes are not necessarily gluten-free as they may contain cereals such as rye, which contain gluten.

CROHN'S DISEASE

People suffering from Crohn's disease often have difficulty absorbing nutrients, and it is essential that they make any changes to their diets under strict medical supervision. Nevertheless, some of the recipes in this book may be useful in cases of known allergies and intolerances.

DIABETES

If you are diabetic do not make any changes to your diet without consulting your doctor.

CHILDREN AND TEENAGERS

Anyone under the age of 18 has greater nutritional requirements than an adult, including a need for vitamins, minerals and trace elements. Serious and irreversible damage can occur, particularly to babies and young children, if they are placed on abnormal diets. The appropriate recipes in this book can, of course, be used once a food allergy or intolerance has been diagnosed.

MOTHERS

Pregnant women and lactating mothers should not undertake any type of exclusion diet. See also page 35.

Basic exclusion diet

The basic exclusion diet is based on avoiding the foods that have commonly been found to provoke the symptoms of food allergy or intolerance. Following a basic exclusion diet is not easy, but most people do manage to complete this three-week diet if they plan and prepare carefully before they begin.

BEFORE YOU START

To help ensure a smooth transition from your ordinary diet to the basic exclusion diet, start your initial planning at least two weeks in advance. The following is a list of things you can do to make your life easier for the duration of the diet:

● Make a list of all the food and drinks you will need on the diet. Some of the items will be rather costly initially, and some foods will be available only from health-food shops or delicatessens. It is worth checking at your supermarket first, however, as some are stocking an increasing range of special dietary products, including soya milk, milk-free margarine and gluten-free biscuits.

● Look at the Basic Exclusion Diet guidelines chart on page 19. If there are any foods listed in the 'Foods allowed' column that you already know affect you adversely – or if you suspect that they do – you should add them to your list of foods to avoid.

● Look through the recipes on pages 38–125 for those that have a basic exclusion diet symbol. You may wish to check the ingredients in your own favourite recipes because some of them may also be suitable. Keep all your recipes together for easy reference.

● For some ideas for fitting the recipes into an eating plan, see the meal plans on pages 37–38.

● Try out a few of the recipes before you actually start the diet. The foods that will seem most different will be foods such as bread, cakes and biscuits, because of the flour mixtures used in their preparation.

● If you have a freezer, stock up in advance on bread and cakes and some pre-prepared meals, especially if you are used to relying on convenience foods. These will be a real asset later on and may even stop you breaking the diet on a day when you are too busy to cook.

● Tell your family and friends that you will be following the diet and explain why you are doing it, so that they do not tempt you to break it.

● Choose a suitable time to start the diet. Avoid times when you will be going away on holiday, for example, or are due to attend an important social function, which may lead you to break the diet.

Exclusion diet meals may be different to the ones you are used to, so it is a good idea to set aside extra time for food preparation and cooking.

It is important to keep a detailed food diary throughout the period you are on the exclusion diet.

If you experience any significant weight loss while on an exclusion diet, you should consult a doctor.

ON THE DIET

When the day comes to start the Basic Exclusion Diet you will appreciate all the work you have put in up to this point. Stay on the diet for exactly three weeks and bear the following points in mind:

● You can use any of the recipes from this book that have a Basic Exclusion Diet symbol, and eat any of the 'allowed' foods listed on page 19.

● See pages 26–34 for help with identifying foods that contain hidden ingredients or derivatives of the foods you are trying to avoid, as well as lists of possible substitutes.

● Remember to continue to keep a detailed diary of your food and symptoms while you are on the diet.

● If you do not keep to the diet, you will have wasted all your earlier efforts and will have to start again. If you fail to complete the diet, you may miss the chance to find out whether your symptoms are food related, and to gain permanent relief from them.

● If any new symptoms, such as weight loss or constipation, occur once you are on the exclusion diet, consult your doctor.

If you do not notice any significant change in your symptoms after three weeks, it is unlikely that food is the cause of your condition. It is possible, however, that the Basic Exclusion Diet contains foods to which you are allergic, in which case you should consider following a Stricter Exclusion Diet (see page 20). You can start this as soon as you have finished the Basic Diet.

If after following the Basic Exclusion Diet for three weeks, you notice significant improvements in your condition, it is likely that your symptoms can be controlled, or improved, in the long term through careful avoidance of the offending foods. You will now be ready to commence stage three, reintroduction (see page 21).

Basic exclusion diet guidelines

		Foods allowed	Foods to avoid
	Meat	Fresh/frozen lamb · pork · beef · chicken · turkey · duck · rabbit · venison	Ham · bacon · smoked meats · salami · canned meats · sausages · burgers and other prepared meat products
	Fish	None	All fish and shellfish
	Milk and milk products	Unsweetened soya milk · oat milk · rice milk · pea protein milk	Cows', goats' and sheep's milks and their products (e.g. yogurt, cheese, cream and butter)
	Eggs	Egg replacer (see page 28)	All eggs · foods containing eggs/egg derivatives (see page 29)
	Fats	Pure oils (e.g. corn, sunflower, olive) · dairy-free margarines	Blended vegetable, sesame or nut oils · dairy-based margarines · butter · suet
	Vegetables	Fresh/frozen vegetables (check ingredients if canned) · pulses	Dried/instant mash · manufactured potato and vegetable products
	Salad	All salad ingredients except those on the forbidden list	Tomato · avocado
	Fruit	All fresh fruit except that on the forbidden list	Kiwifruit · berry fruits · citrus fruits (e.g. oranges, lemons, limes, grapefruit, satsumas)
	Cereals	Corn · rice · oats · barley · rye · sago · buckwheat · millet · tapioca · flours made from these grains · potato flour · gram flour	Wheat and wheat derivatives (see page 30)
	Drinks	Pure juices of permitted fruits · mineral water · soda water · vodka · white rum · camomile tea · peppermint tea	Tomato juice · citrus juices · carbonated drinks · cordials · tea · coffee · alcohol (except that on permitted list)
		Salt · pepper · herbs · spices · jams of permitted fruits · honey · sugar · syrup · treacle	Chewing gum · mouthwash · some medications · chocolate · sweets · manufactured cakes and biscuits

Stricter exclusion diet

Foods to avoid

When you are following the stricter diet, in addition to the foods listed on page 19, you should also avoid:

- ✗ Corn (sweetcorn) and popcorn
- ✗ Oats, barley and rye
- ✗ Onions and leeks
- ✗ Potatoes
- ✗ Seeds, such as sesame seeds, poppy seeds, pumpkin seeds and sunflower seeds
- ✗ Yeast

Rice is the main source of starch on a stricter exclusion diet.

The stricter diet is fundamentally the same as the Basic Exclusion Diet (see pages 17–19) and can be followed if your symptoms remain after the three weeks on the basic diet. It should be started immediately after the Basic Exclusion Diet and continued for no longer than two weeks.

You can use any of the recipes on pages 38–125 that have a stricter exclusion diet symbol. The main starchy foods are rice, rice flour, rice-based breakfast cereals, rice cakes, millet and gram flour (which is derived from various pulses). If there is no improvement in your symptoms after you have followed the stricter diet for two weeks, return to your normal diet and consult your doctor, who may be able to advise you whether more extreme changes to your diet are worthwhile.

If, however, you notice significant improvements after the stricter diet, it is likely that your symptoms can be controlled or improved in the long term if you take steps to avoid the offending foods. You should now proceed to stage three, reintroduction (see page 21).

FURTHER OPTIONS

Although the Basic and Stricter Exclusion Diets discussed in this book are likely to identify problem foods for you, it is possible that you could be allergic or intolerant to some of the foods that you are permitted to eat as part of the diets. Until you have eliminated every single food from your diet, if your symptoms persist, you cannot be sure that they are not food related.

Taking the drastic measures needed in these circumstances will need careful dietary control and should be attempted only under the strict supervision of a dietician. Do not lose heart if the initial diets do not help. Make sure that you take all your food diaries and other relevant information to your dietician to prevent unnecessary repetition. The options your dietician may discuss with you are the 'few foods diet', the 'elemental diet' and 'fasting', although the last option is rarely used because of the potential health risks it poses. All three are extreme and difficult to cope with but are worthwhile if all other avenues have been explored.

Reintroduction

The reintroduction stage is when foods are reintroduced or challenged. The aim of the process is to isolate the culprit foods, and it consists of eating small amounts of the foods to be tested and observing your symptoms. The foods used in the challenges must be in the purest form available (see pages 22–23). At the same time you must continue to keep a food diary. If there is no reaction, gradually increase the amount of that food in your diet.

Once you know that you do not have problems with a particular food, you can return it to your diet. However, if it causes a reaction, you should of course avoid it. All the foods that you continue to avoid can be challenged again at a later stage, before you dismiss them from your diet altogether. Even then, foods that you have previously rejected should be challenged again every six months in case the allergy or intolerance has subsided.

REINTRODUCING FOODS

Follow these guidelines as you reintroduce foods to your diet:

- Excluded foods can by reintroduced in any order.
- Test one new food a week for eczema and migraine. For all other conditions, introduce a new food every third day.
- When reintroducing a food, eat a little more of it every day.
- If you tolerate a food, you can eat it without restriction.
- Foods being reintroduced must be in their purest form. For example, if you plan to reintroduce bread, first you must have reintroduced and tolerated wheat, yeast and any other ingredients found in bread.
- If you want to reintroduce ready-made food but cannot read the food label, do not eat the food.
- If you are unsure whether or not a food is causing a reaction, do not eat it. You can always test it again later.
- If a food provokes a reaction, stop eating it and allow your symptoms to subside completely before testing a new food.

The table overleaf suggests suitable test foods. Take one serving on the first day and, if you tolerate it, increase your intake to two servings on the second day and then three servings on the third day. Reintroduce all other excluded foods in the same way. It is not essential for all the foods in one category to be tested one after another. It may be preferable to reintroduce foods that you eat less often at a later date.

It is important to reintroduce foods individually so that if you experience an adverse reaction, you will know which food has caused it.

Reintroducing foods into your diet

		Suitable test food	Notes
	Wheat	100 per cent wheat pasta · chapattis made with wheat flour · crackers made with 100 per cent wheat	Any foods made from 100 per cent wheat are suitable
	Cows' milk	Cows' milk	If tolerated, try other dairy products one by one
	Yeast	Brewer's yeast tablets · yeast extract	Remember to try these before bread, which contains yeast
	Eggs	Raw egg yolk · raw egg white · cooked egg yolk · cooked egg white	Most mousses and cold soufflés contain raw egg. Very soft-boiled eggs are almost raw
	Coffee	Black instant coffee · black ground coffee (filter, cafetière, espresso)	
	Tea	Black Indian tea · specialized teas (e.g. Earl Grey, orange pekoe) · herbal teas	Herbal teas containing citrus or berry fruits are suitable only if the fruits have been tested first
	Citrus fruits	Orange · lemon · lime · grapefruit · tangerine · mandarin · satsuma	Fresh or frozen citrus fruit are suitable; check labels on canned produce for additives

	Suitable test food	Notes
Fish and shellfish	White fish · oily fish · shellfish	Fresh or frozen fish are suitable; check labels on canned produce for additives
Berry fruits	Blackberry · raspberry · strawberry · loganberry	Fresh or frozen berry fruit are suitable; check labels on canned produce for additives
Chocolate	Cocoa powder · plain dark chocolate	Check ingredients labels for hidden milk derivatives
Nuts	Groundnuts (peanuts) · tree nuts (e.g. walnut, pistachio, almond, hazelnut)	
Alcohol	Beer · wine · spirits · cider	Try organic products first
Potato	Boiled or baked · fried or chipped or crisps	
Preservatives	Most but not all manufactured foods	Choose ready-prepared versions of foods already tested; check labels carefully for additives
Colourings	Coloured sweets	Try boiled sweets

Living on a modified diet

Always check food labels to make sure that the foods you buy do not contain any of the ingredients or derivatives to which you are allergic.

Once you have successfully identified the food or foods that are causing your symptoms or making them worse, you are ready to learn about your new diet, which must exclude all the foods that have produced a reaction. Understanding your diet and following it closely should allow you to remain symptom free or at least much improved.

If you are not already seeing a dietician, obtain a referral from your doctor. It is essential that you understand the nutritional implications of changing your diet and that any potential shortfalls – for example, in your intake of vitamins or protein – are discussed and substitutes found.

The table opposite lists the things you should consider when planning your new diet and suggests ways of making the changes to your lifestyle as smooth as possible.

BUYING SUITABLE FOOD

Buying food and ingredients that are suitable for a modified and restricted diet is getting easier all the time. The food manufacturing industry and supermarkets have improved their labelling over the last decade in accordance with food labelling legislation. They are also voluntarily providing special diet labelling, which is aimed at helping those who wish to eliminate certain foods from their diet. This may be in the form of special coding on the product itself or the foods may have a panel devoted to allergen labelling, for example 'milk free' or 'suitable for a milk-free diet'.

In response to public demand some supermarkets and food manufacturers also produce 'free-from' lists, which are lists of their own-brand products that are suitable for specific diets. They allow the sufferer to identify suitable foods with ease. These are regularly updated and are free of charge.

Ingredients change from time to time, so make sure that you always check the information on the packaging before you buy a product, even if you have used it before.

MANUFACTURED FOODS

Once you have identified the particular food or foods to which you are allergic or intolerant, it is important to follow a special diet accurately to make sure that you are not inadvertently eating derivatives or hidden traces of the foods that cause your problems. This can be particularly difficult when you eat manufactured foods that contain lots of different ingredients, because it can be difficult to know what food derivatives are present when they may appear as an ingredient on a food label under a different guise. See pages 26–34 for information on commonly excluded foods and their derivatives.

Codex Alimentarius, which was set up under the auspices of two United Nations organizations, the World Health Organization and the Food and Agriculture Commission, sets worldwide standards on food issues. (Its website is www.codexalimentarius.net)

Planning your new diet

RECIPES AND REPLACEMENT FOODS
- **Use** the recipes in this book that are coded for your particular diet.
- **Adapt** your own favourite recipes by using alternative foods and ingredients – for example, egg substitutes and alternative flours.
- **Find** and **collect** recipes that do not contain the ingredients you are unable to tolerate.
- **Experiment** with new ingredients and replacement foods.

FOOD LABELS
- **Read** and **understand** food labels so that you can identify suitable and unsuitable foods.
- **Use** manufacturers' and supermarkets' 'free-from' lists, which will help you identify manufactured foods that are suitable for your particular diet and are therefore safe.

BUYING YOUR FOOD
- **Investigate** the wide range of products for special diets stocked in health-food stores.
- **Visit** and order from websites that are dedicated to providing foods for special diets.
- **Join** the relevant associations or self-help groups that have been set up to provide support to people on restricted diets.

AWAY FROM HOME
- **Educate** your friends and family about your new dietary requirements.
- **Eat** regularly in the same restaurants, so they get used to your diet and can provide suitable foods.
- **Be confident** about expressing your dietary needs when you are eating away from home.

Milk

Clockwise from top left: goats' milk butter, soya milk, soya cheese and goats' milk feta cheese.

The term milk includes not only cows' milk but also all related milk-based foods, such as cream, butter and cheese, and items like yogurt, fromage frais and dairy ice cream.

Many processed foods contain milk and dairy products, and these range from obvious foods – milk chocolate and rice pudding, for instance – that are easy to avoid, to products that are hidden sources of milk, which can cause confusion and inadvertent allergic reactions. Examples of hidden sources of milk are casein, which may be found in a packet of biscuits, and lactose, which may be found in the flavouring of crisps.

There are many dairy components you should avoid (see opposite) if you are following a dairy-free diet and you should read all food labels closely so that you can identify and avoid these ingredients.

GOATS' AND SHEEP'S MILK

Although these are not technically dairy products, they have a similar composition to cows' milk and may cause similar reactions. They are, therefore, best avoided if you are following a milk-free diet. Alternatively, reintroduce them by challenge as you do cows' milk, to see if you can tolerate them.

MILK SUBSTITUTES

If you experience an adverse reaction to goats' and sheep's milks in addition to cows' milk, then sample the non-dairy alternatives listed on the opposite page, to find the ones that appeal to you most.

Cheese flavouring

Nutritional yeast flakes are a cheese substitute made from molasses and sold in health-food shops. They are yellow with a sweet, cheese-like taste and are excellent as a flavouring for sauces. These flakes can also be sprinkled as a topping on lasagne or pizza or mixed with mashed potato and cooked in the oven to make a cheese and potato bake. They can also be mixed with a dairy-free margarine, spread on bread and toasted under the grill.

Hidden ingredients

The following may contain milk:
- Batter
- Biscuits
- Bread
- Buns
- Confectionery (sweets and chocolates)
- Crisps
- Ham and other processed meats
- Horseradish sauce
- Muesli
- Packet soups
- Pastry
- Pizza bases
- Potato products (such as hash browns)
- Salami
- Sausages

Foods to avoid

- ✘ Butter · butter oil · buttermilk
- ✘ Casein · caseinate · sodium caseinate · hydrolyzed casein
- ✘ Cheese
- ✘ Cows' or sheep's milk
- ✘ Evaporated, condensed or dried milk
- ✘ Cream
- ✘ Curd
- ✘ Ghee
- ✘ Lactoglobulin
- ✘ Lactose
- ✘ Milk solids
- ✘ Whey · hydrolyzed whey · whey powder · whey syrup sweetener
- ✘ Yogurt

Goats', sheep's or soya milk are all possible alternatives to cows' milk.

Soya products include tempeh (top and centre) and tofu (bottom).

Dairy products	Alternatives
Butter	Soya and dairy-free margarines
Cheese	Soya, rice and tofu cheeses
Cows' milk	Soya, rice, oat, nut and pea milks
Cream	Soya cream, coconut milk
Cream cheese	Soya cream cheese
Ice cream	Soya ice cream, oat ice cream
Yogurt	Soya yogurt, oat yogurt

Eggs

Egg is an ingredient in a wide range of foods and can be difficult to spot.

If you cannot tolerate hens' eggs, you should avoid eggs from all other birds because they are similar in chemical structure and are likely to trigger similar reactions. Cooking eggs denatures many of the egg proteins, which means that some people can safely eat cooked eggs but are unable to tolerate raw eggs.

It is relatively easy to avoid eggs if they are served on their own. However, they are often disguised in prepared and manufactured foods. Read the label carefully to find out if a product contains eggs in any form. If the food does not have a label – many bakery items do not, for example – do not eat it.

EGG SUBSTITUTES

To add variety to your diet when you cannot eat eggs you can follow favourite recipes, but use a whole egg replacer instead of whole egg and egg white replacer instead of egg white. These are available from health-food shops. Instead of using eggs, use an alternative ingredient depending on the eggs' purpose in the recipe – for example, eggs are used as leavening, raising, glazing or binding agents or as a source of liquid. The table opposite indicates suitable alternatives, based on the usual function of the egg in the recipe.

In addition to altering your favourite recipes, try some recipes that are egg-free. These may be recipes that just happen not to include eggs or they may be from a special diet cookbook, a vegan cookbook or the recipes that are supplied with the egg replacer.

Contact the head office of your local supermarket to find out if there is a 'free-from-egg' list, naming the company's own-brand products that are free from egg. This is a free service. Many manufacturers also supply 'free from egg' lists, and you will also find that several products are specially manufactured for those with egg allergies, including cakes, salad dressings, mayonnaise, noodles and fruit and nut bars.

Excluding eggs need not restrict your diet too much if you make use of the ideas above – you may be surprised at how versatile your diet can be without eggs. Many egg-free recipes, such as egg-free cakes or egg-free pancakes, are lower in fat and calories than conventional recipes and may interest friends or family members who wish to reduce the fat or calorie content of their diet.

Hidden ingredients

The following foods may contain eggs:

- Batter
- Cakes
- Coleslaw
- Glaze on bakery products
- Kedgeree
- Lemon curd
- Mousse
- Pâtés
- Pavlova
- Pies and pasties

Foods to avoid

✘ Albumin

✘ Dried egg

✘ Egg (all bird eggs)

✘ Egg powder

✘ Egg protein

✘ Egg white and egg yolk

✘ Frozen egg

✘ Globulin

✘ Lecithin or E322 (this is usually a soya derivative, but can be derived from eggs)

✘ Livetin

✘ Ovalbumin

✘ Ovoglobulin

✘ Ovomucin

✘ Ovovitellin

✘ Pasteurized egg

✘ Vitellin

Suitable alternatives

Purpose of egg in recipe	Alternative ingredients
Leavening	1 tablespoon baking powder + 2 tablespoons liquid
Glazing	Sugar and water or gelatine glaze
Binding	Soya milk, soya dessert, custard, mashed banana, soya cream or white sauce 1 egg = 50 g (2 oz) tofu or 6 tablespoons water + 1 teaspoon arrowroot powder + 2 teaspoons guar gum
Liquid	1 egg = 6 tablespoons apple juice or 4 tablespoons puréed apricot
Raising	1 egg = 1 tablespoon baking powder or ¾ teaspoon bicarbonate of soda + 1 dessertspoon cider vinegar

Egg replacer is a useful ingredient in egg-free baking recipes. It should be sifted into the flour then mixed with the rest of the ingredients.

Wheat

Clockwise from top left: potato flour, buckwheat flour, gram flour, maize meal, millet flour and semolina.

Hidden ingredients

Wheat is used as a processing aid, binder, filler or carrier for flavourings and spices in the following manufactured foods:

- Artificial cream
- Baked beans
- Canned meats
- Dry roasted nuts
- Sweet or savoury pies
- Ketchup
- Muesli
- Mustard
- Packet soups
- Pâtés
- Potato waffles
- Processed cheese
- Sausages
- Suet

WHEAT SUBSTITUTES

If you can tolerate rye, oats, barley, corn and rice, you can include in your diet baked products, cereals and pastas made with these grains instead of their wheat equivalents. In addition, unusual grains and flours, such as millet, quinoa, amaranthus, buckwheat, tapioca, sago, potato, arrowroot, soya, lentil, pea and bean, as well as groundnuts and seeds, can be used in interesting combinations to make baked products and cereals. Many of the commercially available wheat-free products are based on these ingredients. Less readily available and rather more difficult to cook with are sago and tapioca flours. Banana flour and chestnut flour are also available.

Cakes and biscuits made without wheat are rarely entirely successful because they do not rise properly, but they can still be tasty, and in recent years commercial mixes and preparations have improved in quality and have become more widely available. Many of the companies manufacturing these products will send free samples on request, and some products are even available on prescription from your doctor.

GLUTEN

Gluten is the nitrogenous part of cereals such as wheat, rye, barley and oats (see opposite). It is not soluble in water. Coeliac disease is just one of the conditions that requires strict adherence to a gluten-free diet.

Ingredients to be avoided on food labels are these four grains – wheat, rye, barley and oats – as well as alternative names for wheat (see opposite).

Differences between gluten-free and wheat-free diets

A wheat-free diet is a diet that is free from wheat only. A gluten-free diet, on the other hand, is a diet that is free from gluten, which is found not only in wheat but also in barley, rye and oats. However, all these cereals can be eaten on a gluten-free diet if the gluten has been removed. The most common example of this is de-glutenized wheat, which is quite safe for people on a gluten-free diet to eat and is available from health-food shops.

Many of the special products that are manufactured for gluten-free diets are made from de-glutenized wheat. Remember that these are not suitable if you are on a wheat-free diet.

The gluten-free diet and oats

Oats do contain gluten, but it has been found that some people who are unable to tolerate gluten from other cereals are able to tolerate up to 50 g (2 oz) of oats a day. Be sure to discuss the inclusion of oats in your diet with your doctor.

Gluten substitutes

Gluten-free products that are used in place of important basic foodstuffs should supply approximately the same amount of vitamins and minerals as the foods they replace, and they should be prepared with special care so that they are never accidentally cross-contaminated by materials containing gluten.

Gluten- and wheat-free products that are currently available include baking powder, pasta, pizza bases, bakery products, biscuits, cakes, cereal bars, gravy mixes and snack foods. The companies that manufacture these foods will often supply samples on request. This is a good way of trying new foods and finding out which ones you like. Other sources of information on specialized food products include cookery videos and demonstrations. Your dietician will also be able to provide you with useful information.

Foods to avoid

✘ Bran · wheat bran · wheat gluten · wheat germ
✘ Cereal filler · cereal binder · cereal protein
✘ Farina
✘ Flour · wholemeal flour · wheat flour · wheat starch
✘ Rusk
✘ Starch · modified starch · hydrolyzed starch · food starch · edible starch
✘ Vegetable protein · vegetable starch · vegetable gum
✘ Wheat · durum wheat · durum wheat semolina · semolina

Rice cakes (top) and oat cakes (bottom) can make a good substitute for wheat-based snacks.

Seeds can be used in wheat-free baking to add flavour and texture.

Quinoa is a gluten-free cereal and high in protein, calcium and iron.

Fish & shellfish

Many people who suffer from an intolerance to shellfish find that only certain types cause an adverse reaction.

If you are unable to tolerate a particular type of fish or shellfish, it is generally recommended that you avoid all others of this type. The most common fish can be grouped as follows:

- Clam, mussel, oyster, scallop
- Octopus, squid
- Crab, lobster, shrimp, prawn, crayfish
- Ray, shark, skate
- Cod, haddock, plaice, sole
- Salmon, trout
- Mackerel, herring, sardine

Fish is a good source of protein, so if your diet usually contains a lot of fish, it is important to replace it with alternative protein foods, such as meat, eggs, milk and dairy products, nuts and pulses. Excluding fish from your diet is relatively straightforward as sources of fish or shellfish (see left) are usually easy to identify. It is important, however, to check the ingredients of soups, sauces, salad dressings and garnishes as these can contain fish or shellfish.

Hidden ingredients

The following foods contain fish or shellfish:

- Taramasalata
- Worcestershire sauce
- Oyster sauce
- Cod liver oil

Foods to avoid

✘ Anchovy, a small fish from the herring family, is an ingredient of Worcestershire sauce, and is used as a flavour enhancer.

✘ Aspic, a savoury jelly, which may be derived from fish and which is used as a glazing agent.

✘ Caviar, the roe of sturgeon and other fish, which is used as a relish or garnish.

✘ Cod liver oil, the oil extracted from the liver of the cod and related fish, which is often used as a nutritional supplement.

✘ Vitamin D3 (cholecalciferol), a vitamin sometimes derived from fish oil, which is used as a nutritional supplement.

Nuts

Allergy clinics have reported an increase in the incidence of nut and peanut allergies during the 1990s. The exact reasons for this are not known, but it is likely to be related to the increased availability of peanuts and other nuts and their consumption by infants, both directly, in such foods as peanut butter, and indirectly, through the womb and breast-feeding, at a time when their immune systems are not fully developed.

All nuts are potentially dangerous, and it is usually recommended that someone who is allergic to some types of nuts but not others should avoid nuts of all kinds in case they unexpectedly develop an allergy to another type. It is also important to note that peanuts are sometimes used as a cheap substitute for more expensive nuts. They are, for example, washed and treated so that they taste like almonds. Sometimes, they are even crushed and reformed into almond shapes and used for decorating cakes and chocolates.

Refined nut oils are generally suitable for people with nut allergies, but nut oils in the unrefined (crude) form may contain traces of the source nut, so people who are allergic to nuts or peanuts should also avoid these oils. It is not necessary to replace nuts in the diet with an alternative source of protein unless, like vegans and some vegetarians, you rely on them as a major source of protein.

Coconut and nutmeg are not classified as nuts and should be safe to eat for anyone on a nut-free diet. If you prefer to avoid them, then leave them out of recipes or replace them with an alternative ingredient, such as dried fruit.

Nut allergy sufferers have to be particularly careful as nuts are a hidden ingredient in many foods.

Foods to avoid

✗ Hydrolyzed vegetable protein, which may cause an allergic reaction in an extremely sensitive person, is used to add flavour to foods. The source is usually soya or wheat but it can be derived from peanuts or other nuts. (The source does not have to be declared on the label, but some food manufacturers and retailers do so; if you are unsure, contact the manufacturer.)

✗ Hypogeaia (peanut oil)

✗ Peanut flour · nut flour

✗ Peanut protein · nut protein

✗ Unrefined peanut oil · unrefined nut oil

Hidden ingredients

The following foods may contain nuts or traces of nut:

- Biscuits
- Breakfast cereals
- Cakes
- Cereal bars
- Chinese food
- Chocolate bars
- Marzipan
- Nougat
- Pastry
- Satay sauces
- South-East Asian food
- Stuffing
- Vegetarian sausages

Soya

An intolerance to soya can be difficult to identify as it is found in so many foods.

Soya is present in one form or another in many manufactured foods. It is rarely necessary to avoid all the derivatives listed below, which would impose too great a restriction on any diet, but those marked with an asterisk (*) should be avoided.

SOYA SUBSTITUTES

Among the foods that can be eaten by people who cannot tolerate soya milk (or cows' milk) are milks derived from coconut, rice, oats, peas and nuts. These can be homemade or purchased. Vegan cookbooks are a good source of recipes for using these alternative milks or you can purchase a recipe book devoted to milk substitutes.

Soya-free spreads are available; they are usually based on corn, rape seed and sunflower oils. Other foods that can be included in a soya-free and milk-free diet are oat-based cheeses, yogurts and ice creams.

Avoiding soya should not affect the nutritional balance of a diet, unless it is a staple food, as in a vegetarian or vegan diet. It may be possible to replace soya with other pulses, but it is best to do a food challenge (see page 21) before including them in your diet.

Hidden ingredients

Examples of manufactured foods that may contain soya are:

- Bakery products
- Biscuits
- Bread
- Cakes
- Chinese food (contains soy sauce)
- Cold delicatessen meats
- Japanese food (contains miso)
- Teriyaki sauce
- Pâté
- Processed meats
- Seasoned foods
- Vegetarian foods

Foods to avoid

✗ Hydrolyzed vegetable protein
✗ Lecithin · soya lecithin (E322)
✗ Miso*
✗ Soy sauce*
✗ Soya*
✗ Soya albumin
✗ Soya beans*
✗ Soya flour*
✗ Soya milk*
✗ Soya nuts*
✗ Soya oil (especially cold pressed)
✗ Soya protein · soya protein isolate
✗ Soya sprouts*
✗ Soya-based infant formula*
✗ Tempeh*
✗ Textured vegetable protein (TVP)
✗ Tofu*

Pregnancy & parenthood

HEREDITY AND PREGNANCY

If you are planning a family and are concerned about passing on your food allergy or intolerance to your child, discuss your condition with your doctor or allergy specialist. There is now some evidence that avoiding highly allergenic foods, such as peanuts, cows' milk, eggs and wheat, during pregnancy and lactation many help to reduce the incidence of allergy in the unborn child and breast-feeding baby. This is especially important if you are atopic – that is, if you suffer from asthma, eczema, rhinitis or food allergies.

It is important to maintain a balanced diet during pregnancy, however, and following a restricted diet can affect the unborn child if the mother is excluding staple foods from her diet. Any such foods should be replaced by alternatives, and medical advice should be sought to make sure the baby is not being deprived of any vital nutrients.

The most important factor in a child's predisposition to food allergy is a history of allergy in first-degree relatives. Thus, if one or both parents has a food allergy or any other atopic condition – asthma, eczema or hay fever, for example – the probability that the infant will also have an atopic condition increases significantly.

IDENTIFYING ALLERGIES

Parents who suspect that a child has developed an allergy should look for symptoms such as wheezing, lip swelling, eczema, asthma, blocked nose, coughing, hoarseness, itchy eyes, urticarial rash, weals, lumps on the skin, vomiting, diarrhoea and stomach cramps.

WEANING

The order in which foods are introduced into your infant's diet at the weaning stage requires careful planning. As a rule, the least allergenic foods should be introduced first, while those commonly associated with allergic response (milk, eggs, wheat, soya, nuts, citrus fruits, fish and shellfish) should be avoided until the child is at least one year old, when the immune system is more developed. It is important to introduce new foods gradually so that any adverse reaction can be monitored. It is vital that your child has a nutritious, well-balanced diet, so always seek professional advice before you impose any restrictions on your child's foods.

Any foods that you want your child to avoid should be replaced with suitable alternatives. This is particularly relevant to dairy products as these are

Pregnant women should seek medical advice before restricting their diet in any way.

Preparing a packed lunch is a good way of ensuring that an allergic child avoids problem foods, but maintains a balanced diet.

Dried fruit, such as raisins, blueberries and cranberries, makes a tasty and nuritious snack.

an important source of calcium, which is essential for healthy bones, teeth and nails. If your child needs to avoid cows' milk, use soya, rice, peanut or nut, or oat milks instead. Soya or rice cheese can be used to replace regular cheeses, and soya and oat yogurts can be eaten instead of dairy yogurt. Similarly, children excluding meat or fish or following a vegetarian diet, need alternative sources of protein, such as beans and pulses.

Many commercially made snacks are unsuitable for children on a restricted diet so it is important to provide tasty alternatives. The recipes in the Children's party food section (pages 114–125) can be used for parties, lunch boxes and snacks, and will encourage your child to stick to his diet.

STARTING SCHOOL

If your child has a food allergy you should let the school know about this when the child starts school. Preparing a packed lunch may be the best solution as you will be able to control what your child eats during the school day, or you can arrange for the catering staff to be made aware of any special dietary needs. The most appropriate solution will depend on the severity of your child's allergy. Remember also, that cookery may be part of the school curriculum and special arrangements may need to be made for this too.

Requesting the removal of particular foods from the school menu may seem like a good way of helping your child, but it can present other problems. It is important that the child learns how to cope with an allergy and to communicate his specific dietary requirements to other people. Eliminating a food from a school menu can create a false sense of security, by giving the impression that all foods served at school are safe, which may not be the case and may also create problems for other children with different dietary needs. Finally, drawing attention to a child's allergy in this way can lead to bullying or social isolation.

POTENTIAL PROBLEMS FOR CHILDREN

Being extra careful about diet can cause problems for children, including:

- Social stigma or isolation.
- Nutritional deficiencies and weight loss.
- Feelings of inadequacy for the child caused, for example, by parents continually discussing the child's allergy.
- Feelings of deprivation.

The menu plans opposite offer suggestions for ways in which you can include the recipes in this book in your special diet. These plans will help you get started and will show you how varied and appetizing a restricted diet can be for all the family.

Menu Plans

	Breakfast	Lunch	Evening meal
Basic exclusion diet	Honeyed cereal Banana shake	Soya & rice bread sandwiches with chicken breast & cucumber Choc-chip brownies	Italian lamb with broad beans & polenta Totally tropical fruit salad
	Fried liver, potatoes & mushrooms	Wilted Italian salad Jacket potato Exotic pineapple sorbet	Duck with ginger & bamboo shoots Boiled rice Coconut custard tartlets
Stricter exclusion diet	Berry & rice muesli Banana	Super gazpacho Soda bread Gluten-free lemon shortbread	Turkey risotto Mangetout Nectarine
	Soda bread with honey	Spicy coriander & lentil soup Soda bread Fresh fruit tartlet	Fusion-style risotto Wilted Italian salad Totally tropical fruit salad
Vegetarian basic exclusion diet	Power muesli Tofu & exotic fruit shake	Gnocchi with rocket Melon	Quick Thai vegetable curry Boiled rice Exotic pineapple sorbet
	Vegetable fritters Pure apple juice	Spicy cornmeal flatbread Super gazpacho Apple & spice cake	Indian-style dhal Boiled rice Refreshing fruit salad
Vegetarian stricter exclusion diet	Toasted soda bread with honey Banana	Spicy coriander & lentil soup Soda bread Refreshing fruit salad	Vegetable kebabs with fragrant pilaff Fresh fruit
	Berry & rice muesli Pure apple juice	Wilted Italian salad Soda bread Fresh coconut cookies	Fusion-style risotto Green salad Fresh fruit tartlets

	Breakfast	Lunch	Evening meal
Milk-free diet	Power muesli Mixed berry shake	Lentil & okra patties Boiled rice Chocolate & buckwheat cake	Peppered steak with mangetout Chipped potatoes Fruit-filled pancakes with soya ice cream
	Fried bacon, egg & tomato Toast Pure orange juice	Traditional hummus Pitta bread Feta & rocket salad Raspberry & vanilla flan	Chinese griddled fish Noodles Hot choc-chip brownies with soya cream
Egg-free diet	Toasted rice & rye bread with apricot jam	Individual potato pizzas Green salad Crumble jam squares	Oriental pork in hot aubergine sauce Boiled rice Gooseberry & lemon ice cream
	Grilled kippers Toasted soda bread Grapefruit	Herby beefburgers on rocket & spinach salad Chipped potatoes Fresh fruit tartlets	Rustic potato & onion bake Steamed vegetables Mango & lychee ice cream
Wheat-free diet	Power muesli Prunes Pure orange juice	Spicy cornmeal flatbread Indian-style dhal Yogurt	Buckwheat noodles with Bolognese sauce Fruit-filled pancakes
	Fried bacon, mushrooms & tomatoes Soda bread	Feta & rocket salad Herbed polenta Gluten-free lemon shortbread	Garlic-fried spinach with liver Boiled new potatoes Steamed vegetables Fresh fruit tartlets
Gluten-free diet	Berry & rice muesli	Baked potato Beans & peas with tamari dressing Banana	Herby beefburgers on rocket & spinach salad Soya & rice bread Raspberry & vanilla flan
	Fried bacon, eggs & potatoes Pure orange juice	Herb & asparagus salad Lentil & okra patties Coconut custard tartlets	Italian lamb with broad beans & polenta Seasonal fruits

Recipes

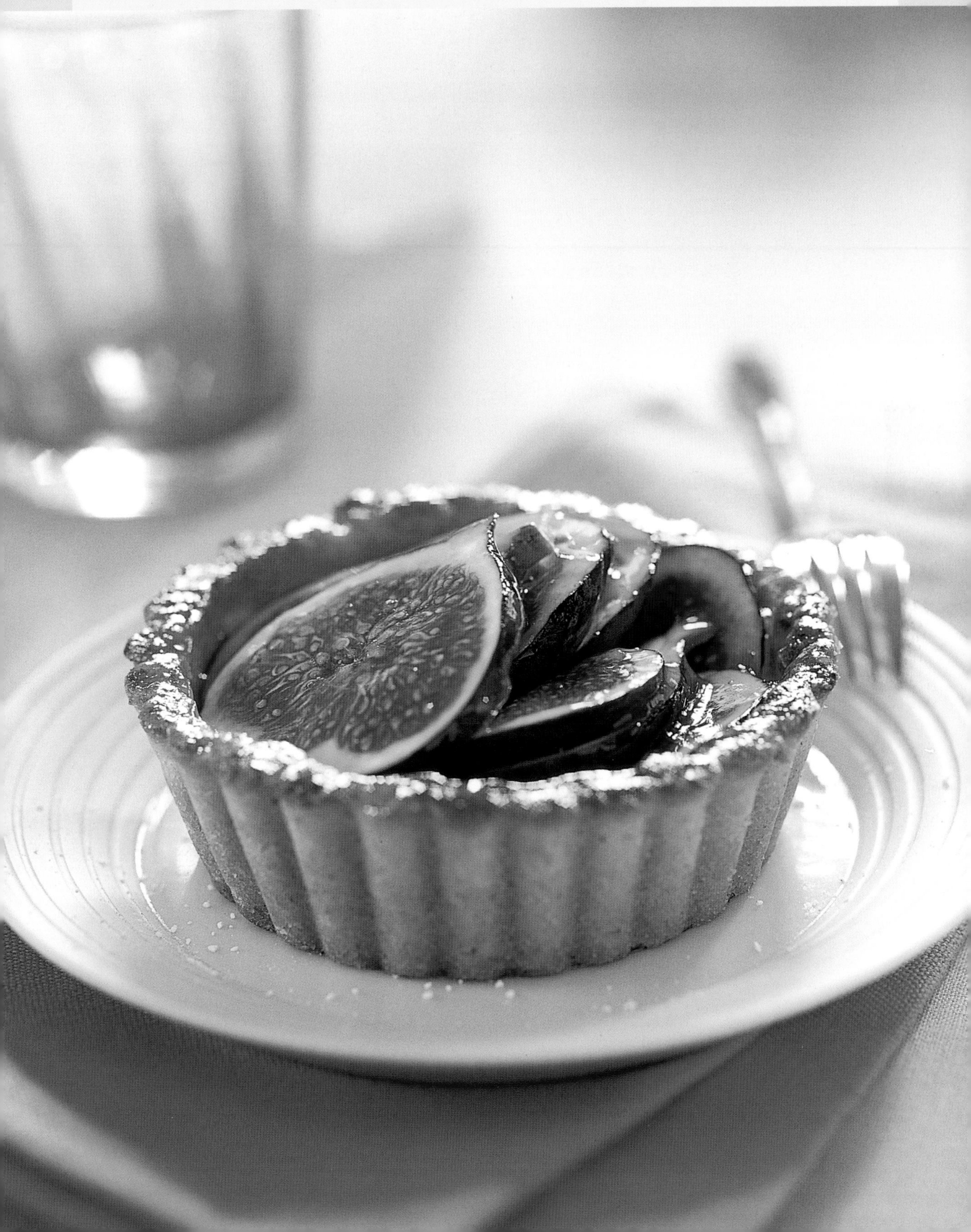

Berry & rice muesli

Serves 4
Preparation: 5–10 minutes

125 g/4 oz brown rice, cooked
50 g/2 oz millet flakes
25 g/1 oz sunflower seeds
50 g/2 oz seedless raisins or sultanas
125 g/4 oz dried strawberries or cranberries
25 g/1 oz desiccated coconut or fresh
grated coconut
milk or milk substitute, to serve

Nutritional Information

Per serving:
Energy 269 kcals/1133 kJ
Protein 5 g
Carbohydrate 46 g
Fat 8 g
Fibre 5 g
Calcium 28 mg
Iron 2 mg

1 Combine all the ingredients, or as many of them as you wish, and put them into an airtight container. The muesli can be stored in the refrigerator for 2–3 days.
2 Serve with milk or milk substitute.

VARIATIONS:

Allowed commercially packaged breakfast cereals may be included instead of the millet flakes.

Power muesli

Serves 10
Preparation: 10 minutes

250 g/8 oz jumbo or rolled oats

125 g/4 oz barley or rye flakes

50 g/2 oz sesame seeds

50 g/2 oz sunflower seeds

125 g/4 oz seedless raisins or sultanas

2 tablespoons wheatgerm

25 g/1 oz pumpkin seeds

250 g/8 oz mixed dried fruit

(apricots, peaches, figs, pears, dates,

nectarines), chopped

Nutritional Information

Per serving:
Energy 308 kcals/1297 kJ
Protein 9 g
Carbohydrate 51 g
Fat 9 g
Fibre 6 g
Calcium 105 mg
Iron 4 mg

1 Combine all the ingredients and store in an airtight container until required.

TIP:

If you keep a vanilla pod in the container with the muesli, it will add a delicate flavour. Serve the muesli with milk, fruit, fruit juice or yogurt.

Honeyed cereal

Serves 12
Preparation: 5 minutes, plus cooling
Cooking: 25 minutes

Nutritional Information

Per serving:
Energy 811 kcals/1311 kJ
Protein 6 g
Carbohydrate 57 g
Fat 7 g
Fibre 3 g
Calcium 59 mg
Iron 2 mg

4 tablespoons sunflower or safflower oil

250 g/8 oz clear honey

250 g/8 oz millet, rye or barley flakes

250 g/8 oz rolled oats

50 g/2 oz sesame seeds

50 g/2 oz dried peaches, banana slices, pears or figs, chopped

125 g/4 oz sultanas or seedless raisins

25 g/1 oz coconut shavings

50 g/2 oz pumpkin seeds

milk or milk substitute, to serve

1 Pour the oil into a roasting tin and heat through. Stir in the honey, flakes, oats and sesame seeds and cook in a preheated oven, 180°C (350°F) Gas Mark 4, for 20 minutes, stirring occasionally so the mixture browns evenly.

2 Remove the tin from the oven. Leave to cool, then mix in the dried fruit, sultanas or raisins, coconut shavings and pumpkin seeds. Store in an airtight container until required.

3 Serve with milk or milk substitute.

TIP:

This cereal mixture also makes a delicious filling for baked apples. If your diet allows, serve it with yogurt, fresh fruit or fruit juice instead of milk or milk substitute. You can also add some nuts if you like.

Banana shake

Serves 2
Preparation: 5 minutes

2 bananas

600 ml/1 pint milk substitute or apple juice

1 tablespoon clear honey, to taste

1 Cut the bananas into small pieces. Put them into a food processor or blender with the milk substitute or apple juice. Add the honey and work to a purée. Pour into chilled glasses and serve at once.

Nutritional Information

Per serving:
Energy 283 kcals/1210 kJ
Protein 2 g
Carbohydrate 72 g
Fat 1 g
Fibre 4 g
Calcium 30 mg
Iron 1 mg

VARIATIONS:

To make the following variations, follow the method for Banana shake using the fruits suggested instead of the bananas.

Mixed berry shake

125 g/4 oz blueberries

75 g/3 oz strawberries, hulled

Mango fruit shake

1 mango, peeled, stoned and roughly chopped

juice of 1 orange

Passion Shake

2 passion fruit, seeds reserved

1 banana, sliced

50 g/2 oz pineapple

Tofu & exotic fruit shake

Serves 4
Preparation: 10 minutes, plus chilling

500 g/1 lb tofu

1 large mango, peeled and roughly sliced

400 g/13 oz can pineapple or lychees with natural juice

3 teaspoons clear honey

natural vanilla extract, to taste (optional)

Nutritional Information

Per serving:
Energy 178 kcals/749 kJ
Protein 11 g
Carbohydrate 23 g
Fat 5 g
Fibre 2 g
Calcium 650 mg
Iron 2 mg

1 Put all the ingredients into a food processor or blender and blend until smooth. Pour into a container and chill until ready to serve.

VARIATIONS:

Vary the choice of fruit as you like. Prunes, peaches, apples, apricots and bananas are all suitable alternatives.

TIP:

You can make a yogurt-like drink by adding water or fruit juice to this fruit shake.

Spicy coriander & lentil soup

Serves 8
Preparation: 10–15 minutes
Cooking: about 2¼ hours

500 g/1 lb red lentils

2 tablespoons vegetable oil

2 onions, chopped

2 garlic cloves, chopped

2 celery sticks, chopped

400 g/13 oz can tomatoes, drained

1 chilli, deseeded and chopped (optional)

1 teaspoon paprika

1 teaspoon harissa paste

1 teaspoon ground cumin

1.2 litres/2 pints vegetable stock or water

salt and pepper

2 tablespoons chopped coriander, to garnish

Nutritional Information

Per serving:
Energy 227 kcals/960 kJ
Protein 15 g
Carbohydrate 36 g
Fat 4 g
Fibre 7 g
Calcium 49 mg
Iron 5 mg

1 Place the lentils in a bowl of water. Heat the oil in a large saucepan and gently fry the onions, garlic and celery over a low heat until softened.

2 Drain the lentils and add them to the vegetable pan with the tomatoes. Mix well. Add the chilli, if using, paprika, harissa paste, cumin and vegetable stock and season with salt and pepper. Cover the pan and simmer gently for about 2 hours, adding a little more vegetable stock or water if the soup gets too thick.

3 Serve the soup immediately in warmed individual bowls topped with a little chopped coriander.

Super gazpacho

Serves 6
Preparation: 20 minutes, plus chilling

Nutritional Information

Per serving:
Energy 78 kcals/324 kJ
Protein 2 g
Carbohydrate 5 g
Fat 6 g
Fibre 2 g
Calcium 26 mg
Iron 1 mg

500 g/1 lb tomatoes, skinned, deseeded and
roughly chopped
2 garlic cloves, chopped
3 tablespoons olive oil
2 tablespoons white wine vinegar or
cider vinegar
600 ml/1 pint water
½ teaspoon sugar
½ cucumber, peeled and roughly chopped
15 g/½ oz basil leaves, roughly torn
salt and pepper

TO GARNISH:
½ cucumber, finely diced
1 small red onion, finely chopped
1 small green and 1 small yellow pepper,
cored, deseeded and finely diced
croûtons made with wheat-/gluten-free bread

1 Put the tomatoes into a food processor or blender with the garlic, olive oil, vinegar, water, sugar, cucumber and basil. Add salt and pepper to taste and process until smooth.
2 Pour the gazpacho into a soup tureen, cover and chill in the refrigerator for at least 2 hours.
3 To serve, put the garnishes into separate small bowls and arrange them around the tureen of gazpacho.

Traditional hummus

Serves 12
Preparation: 15 minutes, plus soaking overnight
Cooking: 1–2 hours

250 g/8 oz dried chickpeas

125 g/4 oz tahini paste

3 tablespoons olive oil

3 garlic cloves, crushed

grated rind and juice of 1 large lemon

salt and pepper

Nutritional Information

Per serving:
Energy 172 kcals/718 kJ
Protein 7 g
Carbohydrate 11 g
Fat 12 g
Fibre 2 g
Calcium 80 mg
Iron 1 mg

TO GARNISH:

6 olives

½ teaspoon pimento piccante or paprika

1 tablespoon olive oil

TO SERVE:

wheat-/gluten-free bread

1 Soak the dried chickpeas overnight in plenty of cold water. The next day, drain them well. Put them into a large pan of water, bring to the boil then reduce the heat and simmer gently until they are tender. This will take between 1–2 hours. Drain well.

2 Place the chickpeas, tahini paste, olive oil, garlic and lemon rind and juice in a food processor or blender with salt and pepper to taste and process for 1 minute. Taste and adjust the seasoning if necessary, then process again briefly.

3 Spoon the hummus into a serving bowl, garnish with olives and sprinkle with pimento piccante or paprika and a little olive oil. Serve with wheat-/gluten-free bread.

TIPS:

For speed and convenience, use canned chick peas and simply drain them in a sieve before putting them in the food processor. For exclusion diets, use 1 tablespoon finely chopped parsley instead of the lemon rind and juice.

Feta & rocket salad

Serves 6
Preparation: 15 minutes

Nutritional Information

Per serving:
Energy 228 kcals/944 kJ
Protein 7 g
Carbohydrate 6 g
Fat 20 g
Fibre 3 g
Calcium 152 mg
Iron 1 mg

6 plum tomatoes, thickly sliced

1 large cucumber, sliced

1 red onion, thinly sliced (optional)

125 g/4 oz feta cheese, broken
into chunks

12–16 black olives

15 g/½ oz rocket or watercress

DRESSING:

4 tablespoons olive oil

2 tablespoons cider vinegar or
lemon juice

1 garlic clove, chopped (optional)

1 tablespoon finely chopped basil
and oregano

salt and pepper

1 Arrange the tomatoes, cucumber, red onion, if using, cheese and olives in a salad bowl.

2 Combine all the ingredients for the dressing in a screw-top jar. Shake until the mixture is pale and smooth, then pour over the salad.

3 Toss the salad well and top with the rocket or watercress.

VARIATION:

This salad serves six as a starter or four as a lunch dish

Italian lamb with broad beans & polenta

Serves 4
Preparation: 10 minutes
Cooking: about 1¼ hours

2 tablespoons olive oil

500 g/1 lb lean boneless leg of lamb,
trimmed and cut into 2.5 cm/1 inch cubes

400 g/13 oz can tomatoes

150 ml/¼ pint water

1 rosemary sprig

1 thyme sprig

1 bay leaf

125 g/4 oz mixed wild mushrooms,
roughly chopped

75 g/3 oz frozen broad beans

salt and pepper

chopped flat leaf parsley, to garnish

Nutritional Information

Per serving:
Energy 280 kcals/1168 kJ
Protein 28 g
Carbohydrate 5 g
Fat 16 g
Fibre 2 g
Calcium 39 mg
Iron 1 mg

1 Heat the oil in a flameproof casserole or heavy-based pan. Add the lamb and cook, stirring frequently, for 5 minutes or until evenly browned. Stir in the tomatoes with their juice and the water. Add the rosemary, thyme and bay leaf and season with salt and pepper to taste. Stir well, then cover the casserole and simmer for 45 minutes.

2 Add the chopped mushrooms and broad beans to the casserole. Taste for seasoning. Cover the casserole and simmer gently for a further 20 minutes.

3 Discard the rosemary, thyme and bay leaf. Sprinkle with chopped parsley and serve with the herbed polenta.

VARIATIONS:

If your diet allows, this dish can also be served with rice or pasta.

Herbed polenta

Serves 4
Preparation: 5 minutes
Cooking: 25 minutes

1.5 litres/2½ pints water

½ teaspoon salt

300 g/10 oz instant or quick-cook polenta

15 g/½ oz dairy-free Parmesan cheese, grated

1–2 tablespoons chopped thyme, rosemary or basil

Nutritional Information

Per slice:
Energy 196 kcals/819 kJ
Protein 6 g
Carbohydrate 36 g
Fat 3 g
Fibre 12 g
Calcium 0 mg
Iron 2 mg

1 Put the water into a large heavy-based saucepan and bring to the boil. Add the salt and reduce the heat so that the water is just simmering.

2 Pour in the polenta in a thin stream, stirring with a wooden spoon. Add the grated Parmesan and chopped herbs, then simmer for 5–10 minutes, stirring constantly to remove any lumps that may form. The polenta is done when it comes away from the sides of the pan as you stir. Pour the cooked polenta on to a large wooden block or a flat dish and leave to cool. When cold, cut it into 1 cm/½ inch thick slices and griddle until lightly browned on both sides.

Oriental pork in hot aubergine sauce

Serves 2
Preparation: 20–30 minutes, plus marinating
Cooking: 10 minutes

Nutritional Information

Per serving:
Energy 380 kcals/1589 kJ
Protein 20 g
Carbohydrate 11 g
Fat 29 g
Fibre 3 g
Calcium 27 mg
Iron 2 mg

175 g/6 oz lean pork, shredded

2 spring onions, finely chopped

1 slice fresh root ginger, finely chopped

1 garlic clove, finely chopped

1 tablespoon tamari wheat-free soy sauce

1½ teaspoons cornflour

600 ml/1 pint corn oil, for deep-frying

250 g/8 oz aubergine, cut into diamond-shaped chunks

1 teaspoon ground pimento piccante or hot paprika

1 tablespoon Tabasco sauce

3–4 tablespoons meat stock, vegetable stock or water

TO GARNISH:

shredded spring onion

shredded ginger

1 Put the pork into a bowl with the spring onions, ginger, garlic, soy sauce and cornflour. Mix well, cover and leave to marinate for about 20 minutes.

2 Heat the oil in a wok or deep-fryer to 180°C (350°F), Gas Mark 4. Lower the heat, add the aubergine chunks and deep-fry for about 1½ minutes. Remove from the pan with a slotted spoon and drain on kitchen paper.

3 Pour off all but 1 tablespoon oil from the pan, then add the pork and pimento piccante or paprika and stir-fry for about 1 minute. Add the aubergine chunks and Tabasco sauce and cook for about 1½ minutes. Moisten with the stock or water and simmer until the liquid has almost completely evaporated. Serve hot, garnished with shredded spring onion and ginger.

Peppered steak with mangetout

Serves 4
Preparation: 10 minutes
Cooking: 10–12 minutes, or according to taste

Nutritional Information

Per serving:
Energy 550 kcals/2300 kJ
Protein 57 g
Carbohydrate 8 g
Fat 34 g
Fibre 5 g
Calcium 72 mg
Iron 6 mg

3 tablespoons sunflower oil

500 g/l lb mangetout or sugar snap peas

1 kg/2 lb fillet or rump steak, cut into 4 pieces

1 tablespoon coarsely ground black pepper

2 teaspoons finely chopped fresh root ginger

1 tablespoon tamari wheat-free soy sauce

coriander leaves, to garnish

1 Heat 1 tablespoon of the oil in a large frying pan. Add the mangetout or sugar snap peas and stir-fry for 2–3 minutes. Transfer to a serving dish and keep hot.

2 Add the remaining oil to the pan. When hot, press the pepper on to one side of each steak and sear for 1 minute or until blood rises on the uncooked surface. Turn the steaks and sear the other side. Remove the steaks from the pan and cut them into 1 cm/½ inch thick strips.

3 Return the steak to the pan with the ginger and soy sauce. Reduce the heat and continue cooking until the steak is cooked to your taste. To serve, arrange the steak on the dish with the mangetout or sugar snap peas and garnish with coriander leaves.

VARIATIONS:

For exclusion diets use pork or turkey fillets instead of beef.

Garlic-fried spinach with liver

Serves 3
Preparation: 10 minutes
Cooking: about 5 minutes

Nutritional Information

Per serving:
Energy 390 kcals/1633 kJ
Protein 32 g
Carbohydrate 22 g
Fat 20 g
Fibre 7 g
Calcium 294 mg
Iron 21 mg

375 g/12 oz pigs' liver, cut into thin triangular slices

2 tablespoons cornflour

4 tablespoons sunflower oil

500 g/1 lb spinach, including stalks, washed and well drained

2 garlic cloves, crushed

5 cm/2 inch piece fresh root ginger, peeled and shredded

½ teaspoon dried chilli flakes

1 tablespoon tamari wheat-free soy sauce

shredded spring onion, to garnish

1 Blanch the liver for a few seconds in boiling water, drain and coat with the cornflour, shaking off any excess.

2 Heat half the oil in a wok or large frying pan. Add the spinach and crushed garlic and stir-fry for 2 minutes. Remove from the pan, arrange in a serving dish and keep hot.

3 Heat the remaining oil in the wok until it reaches smoking point. Add the ginger, liver, dried chilli and soy sauce. Stir-fry quickly for about 1 minute, until the liver is evenly browned, then tip over the spinach.

4 Serve immediately, garnished with shredded spring onion.

Chinese griddled fish

Serves 6
Preparation: 15 minutes, plus marinating
Cooking: 5–10 minutes

Nutritional Information

Per serving:
Energy 176 kcals/740 kJ
Protein 31 g
Carbohydrate 2 g
Fat 5 g
Fibre 0 g
Calcium 36 mg
Iron 1 mg

6 thick pieces of white fish,
about 175 g/6 oz each
2 tablespoons tamari wheat-free soy sauce
2 slices fresh root ginger, peeled and chopped
¼ teaspoon five-spice powder
2 tablespoons sunflower oil
pinch of sugar
pinch of pepper
bunch of spring onions, trimmed
coriander sprigs, to garnish
plain boiled rice, to serve

1 Wipe the fish and remove any visible scales or bones. Combine the soy sauce, ginger, five-spice powder, sunflower oil, sugar and pepper in a shallow dish. Place the fish in the dish and turn to coat thoroughly in the marinade. Leave for 1 hour, turning the fish once.

2 Heat a griddle pan and place the fish on it, skin side up, with the trimmed spring onions. Cook for 4–5 minutes, turning the spring onions frequently.

3 Drizzle the marinade over the fish and cook for a further minute or until the fish is just cooked.

4 Serve the fish with plain boiled rice and topped with the griddled spring onions and the coriander sprigs.

Turkey risotto

Serves 4
Preparation: 10 minutes
Cooking: 25–30 minutes

Nutritional Information

Per serving:
Energy 468 kcals/1980 kJ
Protein 38 g
Carbohydrate 70 g
Fat 6 g
Fibre 3 g
Calcium 31 mg
Iron 1 mg

1 tablespoon olive oil

1 onion, finely chopped

2 garlic cloves, crushed

375 g/12 oz cooked turkey

15 g/½ oz dried porcini mushrooms, soaked
in hot water

50 g/2 oz garden peas

300 g/10 oz Italian arborio rice

1.25 litres/2½ pints vegetable or turkey stock

salt and pepper

1 tablespoon roughly chopped basil,
to garnish

1 Heat the oil in a large frying pan and gently fry the onion for about 5 minutes.
Add the crushed garlic, turkey, mushrooms and their soaking liquid, garden peas
and rice and season with salt and pepper. Fry gently for a further 1–2 minutes,
stirring to coat the all the ingredients well.

2 Heat the stock in a saucepan and keep it simmering on a back burner. Add
150 ml/¼ pint simmering stock to the rice mixture and continue to cook, stirring,
until the rice absorbs the liquid, scraping the rice down the sides of the pan as
you stir. Add another 150 ml/¼ pint of simmering stock and continue adding the
stock until the rice is cooked. It should be fluffy and tender. Add the chopped
basil and serve immediately with a crisp salad.

Duck with ginger & bamboo shoots

Serves 4
Preparation: 10–15 minutes, plus marinating
Cooking: 5–10 minutes

Nutritional Information

Per serving:
Energy 268 kcals/1186 kJ
Protein 18 g
Carbohydrate 3 g
Fat 22 g
Fibre 1 g
Calcium 48 mg
Iron 3 mg

2 tablespoons tamari wheat-free soy sauce

1 tablespoon black bean or hoisin sauce

5–6 slices fresh root ginger, peeled
and shredded

500 g/1 lb duck meat, cut into julienne strips

2½ tablespoons sunflower oil

3 spring onions, cut into matchsticks

200 g/7 oz can bamboo shoots, drained

1 tablespoon cornflour

3 tablespoons water

handful of purple basil leaves

brown rice or noodles, to serve

1 In a large bowl, mix together the soy sauce, black bean or hoisin sauce and ginger, then add the duck meat. Stir and turn until well blended and leave for 30 minutes.

2 Heat the oil in a wok or frying pan over a high heat. Add the meat and ginger mixture and stir-fry for 2 minutes. Add the spring onions and bamboo shoots.

3 Blend the cornflour with the water and add to the wok. Stir and turn for 1 minute, then add the purple basil leaves, stir again and transfer to a warmed serving dish. Serve with brown rice or noodles.

Herby beefburgers on rocket & spinach salad

Serves 6
Preparation: 10–15 minutes
Cooking: 10 minutes

Nutritional Information

Per serving:
Energy 286 kcals / 1186 kJ
Protein 18 g
Carbohydrate 3 g
Fat 22 g
Fibre 1 g
Calcium 48 mg
Iron 3 mg

Ravigote dressing

150 ml/5 fl oz Vinaigrette
dressing (see page 74)
2 tablespoons finely
chopped onion
½–1 tablespoon chopped,
rinsed capers
1 tablespoon chopped parsley
½ teaspoon chopped chervil
½ teaspoon chopped tarragon

Serves 6
Preparation: 5–10 minutes

1 To make the dressing, blend
all the ingredients together in
a small bowl.

500 g/1 lb lean beef, minced
1 onion, finely chopped
1 rosemary sprig,
finely chopped
1 teaspoon Worcestershire
sauce
1 garlic clove, crushed
1 tablespoon chopped parsley
50 g/2 oz rocket
50 g/2 oz baby spinach leaves
salt and pepper
Ravigote dressing (see box)
Tomato sauce (see page 76),
to serve

1 Put the beef into a bowl and add the onion. Stir in the chopped
rosemary, Worcestershire sauce, garlic and parsley. Season well
with salt and pepper and form into 6 patties. Cook for 3–5 minutes
on each side, either in a hot nonstick frying pan, without fat, or
under a preheated grill.
2 Serve the beefburgers on a bed of rocket and spinach leaves and
drizzle with ravigote dressing. Serve the tomato sauce on the side.

VARIATIONS:

If you prefer, use lamb or turkey instead of beef.

Buckwheat noodles with Bolognese sauce

Serves 4
Preparation: 30–40 minutes
Cooking: 2¾–3¼ hours

Nutritional Information

Per serving:
Energy 493 kcals/2058 kJ
Protein 27 g
Carbohydrate 60 g
Fat 18 g
Fibre 2 g
Calcium 52 mg
Iron 5 mg

1 To make the Bolognese sauce, heat the oil in a heavy-based saucepan and gently fry the onion for about 5 minutes until just translucent. Add the celery and carrots and cook for a further 2 minutes.

2 Add the meat, breaking it up with a fork. Season to taste with salt and pepper and cook until the meat has browned.

3 Add the tomatoes, chopped courgettes and nutmeg and stir thoroughly. When the tomatoes start to bubble, turn the heat down and simmer, uncovered, for 2½–3 hours until the sauce is cooked. If the sauce gets too dry, add a little water.

4 To make the noodles, put the flour, egg replacer mixture and oil in a bowl with a pinch of salt. Mix thoroughly, then add the water, a little at a time, to make a thick, fairly stiff dough. Alternatively, put all the ingredients into a food processor and blend until they come together to form a ball. Knead well.

5 Lightly flour the work surface and roll out the dough thinly. Cut it into noodles.

6 Bring a large saucepan of lightly salted water to the boil. Add the noodles and boil for 3–5 minutes. Drain the noodles thoroughly and transfer to a warmed serving dish. Place the Bolognese sauce on top and serve immediately.

TIP:

The Bolognese sauce can be made in large quantities and frozen, or stored in the refrigerator for up to 5 days.

VARIATION:

If you prefer, use minced pork instead of beef, or 175 g/6 oz minced beef and 175 g/6 oz minced pork.

BOLOGNESE SAUCE:

3 tablespoons olive oil

1 small onion, chopped

1 celery stick, chopped

2 carrots, chopped

375 g/12 oz lean
minced beef

400 g/13 oz can tomatoes,
chopped, with their juice

2 courgettes, chopped

pinch of grated nutmeg

salt and pepper

BUCKWHEAT NOODLES:

250 g/8 oz buckwheat flour

2 teaspoons egg
replacer mixed with 4
tablespoons water

1 tablespoon sunflower oil

4–5 tablespoons water

salt

Quick Thai vegetable curry

Serves 4
Preparation: 10–15 minutes
Cooking: 35–45 minutes

2 tablespoons sunflower oil

1 onion, chopped

2 garlic cloves, crushed

5 cm/2 inch piece of fresh root ginger, peeled and grated

1½ tablespoons Thai red curry paste

600 ml/1 pint vegetable stock

3 kaffir lime leaves

250 g/8 oz sweet potatoes, peeled and diced

250 g/8 oz pumpkin, peeled, deseeded and cubed

8 baby corn cobs, trimmed

1 aubergine, roughly chopped

125 g/4 oz green beans, chopped

125 g/4 oz small button mushrooms

200 g/7 oz can bamboo shoots, drained

salt and pepper

plain boiled jasmine or brown rice, to serve

Nutritional Information

Per serving:
Energy 188 kcals/788 kJ
Protein 5 g
Carbohydrate 21 g
Fat 10 g
Fibre 5 g
Calcium 79 mg
Iron 3 mg

TO GARNISH:

1 tablespoon grated fresh coconut

handful of Thai basil leaves

1 Heat the oil in large saucepan. Add the onion, garlic and ginger and fry gently for 5 minutes, stirring occasionally. Stir in the Thai red curry paste and fry gently for a further 3 minutes, stirring constantly.

2 Add the stock and kaffir lime leaves and bring to the boil, add salt and pepper to taste, then lower the heat and simmer for 2 minutes. Add the sweet potatoes and pumpkin, cover the pan and simmer for 10 minutes.

3 Add the baby corn, aubergine, green beans, mushrooms and bamboo shoots, replace the lid and simmer for a further 5–10 minutes or until the beans are just tender but still crisp.

4 Taste and adjust the seasoning. Turn the curry into a warmed serving dish and sprinkle with the coconut and basil leaves. Serve with the rice.

Indian-style dhal

Serves 4
Preparation: 10 minutes
Cooking: 30–45 minutes

250 g/8 oz red lentils

600 ml/1 pint water

1 bay leaf

1 tablespoon sunflower oil

1 onion, finely chopped

1 garlic clove, crushed

2 teaspoons grated fresh root ginger

½ teaspoon ground coriander

½ teaspoon ground cumin

½ teaspoon black onion seeds

½ teaspoon ground turmeric

juice of 1 lime

salt and pepper

Nutritional Information

Per serving:
Energy 233 kcals/987 kJ
Protein 15 g
Carbohydrate 37 g
Fat 4 g
Fibre 7 g
Calcium 39 mg
Iron 5 mg

TO SERVE:

2 tablespoons coconut milk

handful of coriander leaves

1 Place the lentils in a saucepan, add the water and bay leaf and season with salt and pepper. Bring to the boil then cover the pan and simmer for 15–30 minutes until the lentils have formed a thickish purée.

2 Heat the oil in another pan and fry the onion, garlic and ginger for 5 minutes until lightly browned. Add the coriander, cumin, onion seeds and turmeric and fry for 1 minute. Stir in the lentil purée and cook gently for 5 minutes.

3 Just before serving, add the lime juice and taste for seasoning. Serve the dhal drizzled with coconut milk and topped with coriander leaves.

VARIATIONS:

This dhal can be served hot with chappati and plain rice, or as an accompaniment to a curry or cold with a salad.

Lentil & okra patties

Serves 6
Preparation: 10–15 minutes
Cooking: about 1½ hours

2 tablespoons sunflower oil, plus extra for shallow frying

½ fennel bulb, about 125 g/4 oz, chopped

50 g/2 oz celeriac, peeled and chopped

4 okra, trimmed and diced

1 carrot, chopped

250 g/8 oz brown lentils

450 ml/¾ pint water

4 tablespoons gram flour

½ teaspoon ground ginger

½ teaspoon ground coriander

¼ teaspoon cumin seeds

1 teaspoon wheat-free curry powder

2 tablespoons chopped parsley or coriander

salt and pepper

Nutritional Information

Per serving:
Energy 230 kcals/978 kJ
Protein 14 g
Carbohydrate 29 g
Fat 8 g
Fibre 4 g
Calcium 108 mg
Iron 7 mg

TO SERVE:

plain boiled rice

mango chutney

Tomato sauce (see page 76)

1 Heat 2 tablespoons of the oil in a large pan. Add the fennel, celeriac, okra and carrot and fry gently until they begin to soften.

2 Add the lentils and water and season with salt and pepper. Bring to the boil, then lower the heat, cover the pan and simmer for about 1 hour until the lentils are soft and all the liquid is absorbed.

3 Add half the flour, the ginger, ground coriander, cumin, curry powder and chopped parsley or coriander to the pan and mix well. Continue to cook gently for 2–3 minutes, stirring constantly.

4 Turn the mixture on to a plate and leave until cool enough to handle. Divide it into 18 pieces and form each one into a patty, about 1 cm/½ inch thick. Coat the patties with the remaining flour. Heat a little oil in a frying pan and fry the patties, a few at a time, until crisp and golden brown, turning once.

5 Serve the patties on a bed of rice topped with the mango chutney or Tomato sauce with a dash of Tabasco.

Vegetable kebabs with fragrant pilaff

Serves 4
Preparation : 15–20 minutes
Cooking: 30–35 minutes

Nutritional Information

Per serving:
Energy 446 kcals/1880 kJ
Protein 9 g
Carbohydrate 81 g
Fat 12 g
Fibre 10 g
Calcium 99 mg
Iron 4 mg

PILAFF:

2 tablespoons sunflower oil

1 large onion, chopped

2 celery sticks, sliced

250 g/8 oz brown rice

600 ml/1 pint vegetable stock

50 g/2 oz dried sour cherries
or seedless raisins

50 g/2 oz dried apricots,
roughly chopped

1 cinnamon stick

6 whole cloves

6 cardamom pods, bruised

1 bay leaf

salt and pepper

KEBABS:

250 g/8 oz courgettes, sliced

8 cherry tomatoes

1 large red or sweet onion, cut
into wedges

8 button mushrooms

1 green pepper, cored,
deseeded and cut into 8 pieces

4 black olives

1 tablespoon olive oil

1 teaspoon sun-dried
tomato purée

1 tablespoon thyme leaves

fresh coriander, to garnish

1 To make the pilaff, heat the oil in a saucepan. Add the onion and celery and fry gently for 5 minutes until golden brown. Add the rice and cook for 1 minute, stirring constantly. Pour in the stock, then add the sour cherries or raisins and apricots. Bring to the boil, stirring occasionally, then add the cinnamon, cloves, cardamoms and bay leaf and season with salt and pepper. Lower the heat, cover the pan and simmer for 30 minutes or according to packet instructions until the rice is tender and the stock has been completely absorbed.

2 Meanwhile, to make the kebabs, blanch the courgettes in boiling water for 1 minute, then drain well. Thread the vegetables alternately on to 4 large, metal kebab skewers ending with the black olives.

3 Mix the oil with the sun-dried tomato purée and thyme and season to taste with salt and pepper, then brush over the vegetables. Cook the kebabs on a barbecue or under a preheated grill for 5–10 minutes until cooked through, turning and basting them from time to time.

4 Spoon the pilaff into a warmed shallow serving dish and arrange the kebabs on top, garnished with the coriander.

Individual potato pizzas

Serves 4
Preparation: 10–15 minutes
Cooking: 30–40 minutes

Nutritional Information

Per serving:
Energy 413 kcals/1724 kJ
Protein 11 g
Carbohydrate 38 g
Fat 25 g
Fibre 5 g
Calcium 99 mg
Iron 1 mg

750 g/1½ lb potatoes, grated

4 tablespoons extra virgin olive oil

4 tablespoons sun-dried tomato purée

1 garlic clove, crushed

2 spring onions, chopped

8 cherry tomatoes, halved

1 small red or green pepper, cored, deseeded and chopped

175 g/6 oz goats' cheese, crumbled

4 small rosemary sprigs

salt and pepper

1 Squeeze the grated potatoes in kitchen paper to remove any excess juice.

2 Heat the oil in a heavy-based frying pan and add a quarter of the potato. Flatten it into a circle (not quite the diameter of the pan, for easy turning) and cook for a few minutes until the base is crisp and golden. Turn over and cook the other side. When cooked, place the pizza base on a large baking sheet. Cook the other three pizza bases in the same way.

3 Mix the sun-dried tomato purée with the garlic and spread evenly over the potato bases, extending it right out to the edges. Scatter the spring onions over the bases and add the cherry tomatoes, red or green pepper, goats' cheese, rosemary and salt and pepper.

4 Place the pizzas under a hot grill for 5–10 minutes or until they are hot and the goat's cheese is beginning to melt. Serve immediately.

VARIATIONS:

The key consideration here is the wheat-free base. You can vary the toppings according to taste.

Fusion-style risotto

Serves 4
Preparation: 10–15 minutes
Cooking: about 45 minutes

Nutritional Information

Per serving:
Energy 445 kcals/1877 kJ
Protein 14 g
Carbohydrate 74 g
Fat 13 g
Fibre 8 g
Calcium 180 mg
Iron 3 mg

2 tablespoons olive oil

2 large onions, sliced

2 garlic cloves

175 g/6 oz butternut squash, peeled and chopped

1 fennel bulb, about 250 g/ 8 oz, chopped

250 g/8 oz Italian arborio rice

600 ml/1 pint vegetable stock

1 bay leaf

1 aubergine, about 250 g/ 8 oz, diced

125 g/4 oz shiitake mushrooms, sliced

125 g/4 oz frozen peas

125 g/4 oz firm tofu, cubed

salt and pepper

chopped parsley, to garnish

olive oil, to serve

1 Heat the oil in a large heavy-based frying pan, add the onions, garlic, butternut squash and fennel and fry gently for 10 minutes without browning, stirring frequently. Stir in the rice and cook for 3–4 minutes. Add the stock and bay leaf and season with salt and pepper. Bring to the boil, stirring occasionally, then cover the pan and simmer for 15 minutes.

2 Add the aubergine and mushrooms and stir well. Cover the pan and continue simmering for 10 minutes, stirring occasionally. Stir in the peas, adding a little boiling water if all the liquid has been absorbed.

3 Add the tofu and continue cooking for 5–10 minutes or until the rice is tender and all the liquid has been absorbed. Taste and adjust the seasoning and discard the bay leaf.

4 Pile the risotto on to a hot serving dish and garnish with parsley. Serve drizzled with a little olive oil.

VARIATIONS:

You can change the vegetable ingredients of this risotto according to your taste, adding courgettes, fresh or canned tomatoes, French or runner beans, nuts, peppers or pre-soaked pulses. Amend the cooking time if necessary. A green salad makes a good accompaniment.

Herb & asparagus salad

Serves 8
Preparation: 10 minutes
Cooking: 5 minutes

1 garlic clove, halved

1 Cos lettuce, roughly torn

125 g/4 oz lamb's lettuce

1 bunch of watercress

1 punnet of mustard and cress

1 bunch of rocket

1 small bunch of chervil

1 bunch of chives

1 bunch of flat leaf parsley

1 bunch of basil

1 bunch of mint

1 avocado, peeled, stoned and
roughly chopped

175 g/6 oz young asparagus

Nutritional Information

Per serving:
Energy 78 kcals/323 kJ
Protein 2 g
Carbohydrate 2 g
Fat 7 g
Fibre 1 g
Calcium 50 mg
Iron 1 mg

DRESSING:

2 tablespoons olive oil

1 tablespoon white wine or
tarragon vinegar

2 garlic cloves, crushed

¼ teaspoon soft
brown sugar

¼ teaspoon sweet paprika

1 Use the cut garlic clove to rub round the inside of a large bowl, then discard.

2 Wash and prepare the salad greens, using as many as are available. Chop the chives and parsley and strip the leaves from the basil and mint, discarding the stems. Place the salad greens and herbs in the salad bowl with the chopped avocado and mix well.

3 Heat a griddle pan, add the asparagus in a single layer and cook for 5 minutes, turning constantly, until charred and beginning to soften.

4 To make the dressing, place all the ingredients in a bowl and whisk together, or place in a screw-top jar and shake well.

5 Just before serving put the hot asparagus on the top of the salad, pour the dressing over the salad and toss well.

Wilted Italian salad

Serves 4
Preparation: 10–15 minutes
Cooking: 10 minutes

Vinaigrette dressing

150 ml/¼ pint oil
5 tablespoons cider, white wine or balsamic vinegar
1 garlic clove (optional)
1 teaspoon wheat-free French mustard
1 herb sprig (optional)
1 teaspoon clear honey
pinch of paprika (optional)
salt and pepper

Makes 200 ml/7 fl oz
Preparation: 5 minutes

1 Put all the ingredients into a screw-top jar and shake well to mix.
2 Store in the refrigerator and use as required, dressing salads just before serving.

VARIATIONS: Use corn, sunflower or safflower oil or, for a stronger flavour, use olive oil.

10 baby plum tomatoes, halved
1 tablespoon balsamic vinegar
1 fennel bulb, sliced into rings
½ head curly endive, separated into leaves
1 head chicory, sliced into rings
1 small head radicchio, separated into leaves and shredded
8 radishes, thickly sliced
½ tablespoon capers
8 black olives
handful of basil leaves
4 tablespoons Vinaigrette dressing (see box)
salt and pepper

1 Place the plum tomatoes under a preheated grill or on a griddle and cook until soft and lightly charred. Sprinkle with the balsamic vinegar and salt and pepper.
2 Grill or griddle the fennel, then put the tomatoes and fennel into a large salad bowl.
3 Put the endive, chicory, radicchio, radishes, capers, black olives and basil leaves on top of the warm vegetables. Drizzle with the vinaigrette, toss thoroughly and serve at once.

Nutritional Information

Per serving:
Energy 104 kcals/429 kJ
Protein 2 g
Carbohydrate 4 g
Fat 9 g
Fibre 2 g
Calcium 44 mg
Iron 2 mg

Gnocchi with rocket

Serves 6
Preparation: 10–15 minutes
Cooking: about 30 minutes

750 g/1½ lb King Edward, Maris Piper or
other potatoes suitable for mashing, unpeeled
50 g/2 oz potato flour
50 g/2 oz buckwheat flour
salt

TO GARNISH:
rocket leaves
dairy-free margarine or extra virgin olive oil
chopped flat leaf parsley or basil

Nutritional Information

Per serving:
Energy 187 kcals/787 kJ
Protein 4 g
Carbohydrate 35 g
Fat 4 g
Fibre 3 g
Calcium 27 mg
Iron 1 mg

1 Boil the unpeeled potatoes in a large pan of water. Drain and leave to cool slightly. Peel them as soon as they are cool enough to handle. Purée while still warm and add salt to taste.

2 Gradually add the potato flour and buckwheat flour to the potato purée and knead. The dough should be smooth and still slightly sticky. You may not need to add all the flour.

3 Shape the dough into tiny sausages and press one side gently with the prongs of a fork to make a pattern. Drop the gnocchi into a pan of boiling water and cook for 3–5 minutes after they have risen to the surface.

4 Drain the gnocchi and serve on a bed of rocket leaves. Dot with margarine or drizzle with olive oil and sprinkle with parsley or basil.

Vegetable fritters

Serves 8
Preparation: 15 minutes, plus draining the aubergines
Cooking: 20 minutes

Nutritional Information

Per serving:
Energy 164 kcals/689 kJ
Protein 4 g
Carbohydrate 24 g
Fat 6 g
Fibre 3 g
Calcium 20 mg
Iron 1 mg

Tomato Sauce

1 tablespoon corn oil
1 onion, chopped
400 g/13 oz can peeled plum tomatoes, with juice
2 teaspoons Worcestershire sauce
1 teaspoon raw cane sugar
1 tablespoon cornflour or potato flour
150 ml/¼ pint water
pinch of salt

Preparation: 5 minutes
Cooking: about 20 minutes

1 Heat the oil in a frying pan and fry the onion for about 5 minutes. Add the tomatoes and Worcestershire sauce.
2 Mix the sugar with the flour, blend with a little of the water and add to the pan with the remaining water and the salt.
3 Bring to the boil and simmer for 10 minutes, stirring occasionally.

50 g/2 oz potato flour
50 g/2 oz brown rice flour
pinch of salt
2 teaspoons egg replacer
150 ml/¼ pint water or milk substitute
1 small aubergine, sliced
2 courgettes, thinly sliced
8 onion rings
8 cauliflower florets
16 basil leaves
8 asparagus spears
1 raw beetroot, peeled and thickly sliced

1 red pepper, cored, deseeded and cut into thin rings
corn oil, for deep-frying
Tomato sauce (see box) or tamari wheat-free soy sauce, to serve

1 First make the batter. Sift the flours and a pinch of salt into a bowl and make a well in the centre. Add the egg replacer and gradually add the water or milk substitute, whisking until the batter is smooth.
2 Place the aubergine slices in a colander, sprinkle with salt and leave to drain for 30 minutes. Rinse and dry well on kitchen paper.
3 Working in batches, dip the vegetables in the batter, shake off any excess, and deep fry in hot oil, 180°C (350°F), Gas Mark 4, for 5 minutes, until the vegetables are tender and the batter is crisp. Drain the fritters on kitchen paper and serve immediately with Tomato sauce or soy sauce.

Beans & peas with tamari dressing

Serves 6
Preparation: 10–15 minutes
Cooking: 5–6 minutes

Nutritional Information

Per serving:
Energy 138 kcals/579 kJ
Protein 7 g
Carbohydrate 10 g
Fat 8 g
Fibre 5 g
Calcium 60 mg
Iron 2 mg

500 g/1 lb mangetout, topped and tailed
250 g/8 oz broad beans
125 g/4 oz petit pois
3 spring onions, finely chopped
2 tomatoes, peeled and chopped

TAMARI DRESSING:
3 tablespoons cider vinegar
4 tablespoons sesame or olive oil
1 tablespoon chopped chives
1 tablespoon tamari wheat-free soy sauce
1 parsley sprig, chopped
salt and pepper

1 Place the mangetout, broad beans and petit pois in a saucepan with just enough water to cover them. Bring to the boil, then lower the heat and cook gently for 5–6 minutes, depending on the ripeness and freshness of the mangetout (very young pods will need only about 2 minutes). Drain well and place in a serving dish with the chopped spring onions and tomatoes.
2 To make the dressing, beat together all the ingredients until well blended.
3 Pour the dressing over the vegetables while they are still warm and toss well. Leave to stand for at least 5 minutes before serving, or leave to cool completely and serve cold.

Rustic potato & onion bake

Serves 6
Preparation: 10–15 minutes
Cooking: about 1 hour

2 tablespoons olive oil

2 Spanish onions, roughly chopped

4 tablespoons chopped flat leaf parsley

1 tablespoon capers

4 anchovies, chopped

6 large potatoes, sliced

salt and pepper

Nutritional Information

Per serving:
Energy 180 kcals/767 kJ
Protein 5 g
Carbohydrate 33 g
Fat 5 g
Fibre 4 g
Calcium 32 mg
Iron 1 mg

1 Heat the oil in a frying pan, add the onions and cook for 5 minutes until golden brown. Mix together the chopped parsley, capers and anchovies.

2 Fill an ovenproof dish with alternate layers of sliced potato, the parsley mixture and the fried onions, seasoning each layer with pepper and finishing with a layer of fried onions.

3 Cook in a preheated oven, 190°C (375°F), Gas Mark 5, for 1 hour or until the potatoes are tender. This is a good accompaniment to baked or grilled fish.

Fresh fruit tartlets

Makes 12 tartlets
Preparation: 25 minutes, plus cooling
Cooking: 20 minutes

Nutritional Information

Per serving:
Energy 100 kcals/420 kJ
Protein 1 g
Carbohydrate 16 g
Fat 4 g
Fibre <1 g
Calcium 8 mg
Iron 0 mg

SWEET SHORTCRUST PASTRY:

125 g/4 oz brown rice flour

50 g/2 oz dairy-free hard margarine

75 g/3 oz finely grated cooking apple
or quince

1 teaspoon sugar (optional)

FILLING:

300 g/10 oz blueberries, papaya, Cape
gooseberries, fresh lychees, mango, sharon
fruit or figs, sliced

125 g/4 oz apricot jam (additive-free, sugar-
reduced variety)

1 tablespoon water

Creamy topping (see box), to serve (optional)

1 To make the pastry, put the flour into a bowl and rub in the margarine until it resembles fine breadcrumbs. Add the grated apple or quince and sugar, and knead into a ball.

2 Roll out the pastry to a thickness of 5 mm/¼ inch. Cut out tart cases with a pastry cutter and put them in a greased patty tin. Prick the bases with a fork and fill with baking beans. Place on a baking sheet and bake blind in a preheated oven, 200°C (400°F), Gas Mark 6, for about 15 minutes or until crisp and golden. Remove the baking beans and leave the tartlet cases to cool.

3 When cold, fill the tartlet cases with the sliced fresh fruit.

4 To make a jam glaze, put the jam into a saucepan with the water and heat gently until the jam softens. Push the mixture through a sieve. If the glaze needs to be thicker, return it to the saucepan and boil until it has thickened to a suitable coating consistency.

5 Brush the glaze over the tartlets and serve with creamy topping, if desired.

Creamy topping

25 g/1 oz cornflour
300 ml/½ pint milk substitute
50 g/2 oz dairy-free soft
margarine or goat's butter
25 g/1 oz icing sugar, sifted

Preparation: 5–10 minutes
Cooking: about 10 minutes

1 Blend the cornflour with a little of the milk substitute. Heat the remaining milk substitute in a saucepan and pour on to the blended cornflour. Mix well and return to the pan. Bring to the boil and simmer for 1 minute, stirring all the time.

2 Remove from the heat and leave to cool completely, stirring occasionally.

3 Beat the margarine or butter until soft and gradually work in the icing sugar. Add the milk, a little at a time, beating vigorously to produce a smooth consistency.

VARIATIONS:

Add the finely grated rind of 1 lemon or 1 small orange.

Shortcrust pastry

200 g/7 oz cornflour or sago flour
pinch of salt
100 g/3½ oz dairy-free hard margarine

Preparation: 10 minutes

1 Sift together the flour and salt. Rub in the margarine until the mixture resembles fine breadcrumbs. Add sufficient chilled water to mix until it clings together.

2 Chill for at least 20 minutes, then roll out and use as required. The pastry can be kept in the refrigerator for 2–3 days or frozen for up to 3 months. Thaw frozen pastry thoroughly before using. Use extra flour for rolling out and grease the cooking tins with dairy-free margarine.

Raspberry & vanilla flan

Serves 6
Preparation: 15 minutes, plus chilling and cooling
Cooking: 20 minutes

Nutritional Information

Per serving:
Energy 229 kcals/968 kJ
Protein 5 g
Carbohydrate 33 g
Fat 9 g
Fibre 4 g
Calcium 25 mg
Iron 1 mg

175 g/6 oz Sweet shortcrust pastry (see page 80)

FILLING:
25 g/1 oz cornflour
25 g/1 oz caster sugar
1 egg, beaten
300 ml/½ pint milk substitute
1 teaspoon natural vanilla extract
250 g/8 oz fresh raspberries, hulled

GLAZE:
2 teaspoons arrowroot
150 ml/¼ pint clear apple juice
1 teaspoon sugar

1 Line a 20 cm/8 inch fluted flan ring or flan dish with the pastry and prick the base. Place the dish on a baking sheet and chill for 10 minutes, then line with greaseproof paper and fill with baking beans. Bake blind in a preheated oven, 200°C (400°F), Gas Mark 6, for 20 minutes. Leave to cool.

2 Meanwhile, make the confectioner's custard by blending the cornflour, sugar and egg in a bowl. Gently heat the milk substitute, then pour it on to the mixture, stirring well.

3 Return the mixture to the saucepan, heat until boiling, then simmer for 2 minutes, stirring all the time. Add the vanilla extract, cover with damp greaseproof paper and leave to cool.

4 Spread the cooled custard over the base of the baked flan case. Arrange the raspberries neatly over the custard.

5 To make the glaze, blend the arrowroot with a little apple juice in a bowl. Add the sugar and the remaining juice. Pour the mixture into a saucepan and bring to the boil, stirring all the time until the glaze becomes transparent. Lightly brush over the fruit. Serve the flan chilled.

VARIATION:

This flan can also be made with cherries. Remove the stones before adding them to the flan.

Coconut custard tartlets

Makes 12 tartlets
Preparation: 15 minutes, plus cooling and setting
Cooking: 20 minutes

Nutritional Information

Per serving:
Energy 100 kcals/426 kJ
Protein 2 g
Carbohydrate 18 g
Fat 5 g
Fibre 1 g
Calcium 5 mg
Iron 0 mg

250 g/8 oz Sweet shortcrust pastry (see page 80)
450 ml/¾ pint milk substitute
1 vanilla pod
3 teaspoons egg replacer
1 teaspoon clear honey (optional)
freshly grated coconut, grated nutmeg, slices of strawberry, a few blueberries or thin slices of lemon, to decorate

1 Roll out the pastry to a thickness of 5 mm/¼ inch and cut out 5 cm/2 inch tartlet cases with a pastry cutter. Put them in a greased patty tin, prick the bases and fill with baking beans. Bake blind in a preheated oven, 200°C (400°F), Gas Mark 6, for 15 minutes until crisp and golden. Remove the baking beans and leave to cool.

2 Pour the milk substitute into a saucepan, add the vanilla pod and bring to the boil, then leave to cool slowly. Remove the vanilla pod.

3 Mix 4 tablespoons of the vanilla-flavoured milk substitute with the egg replacer, then add the remaining milk substitute. Stir in the honey, if using. Return the mixture to the saucepan and cook, stirring, for 2–3 minutes, then leave to cool slightly.

4 Fill the tart cases with the custard and leave to set.

5 To serve, sprinkle the individual tarts with a little freshly grated coconut or nutmeg or top with sliced strawberries, a few blueberries or slices of lemon.

Gooseberry & lemon ice cream

Serves 5
Preparation: 20 minutes, plus freezing
Cooking: about 20 minutes

Nutritional Information

Per serving:
Energy 90 kcals/388 kJ
Protein 3 g
Carbohydrate 17 g
Fat 2 g
Fibre 0g
Calcium 50 mg
Iron 1 mg

750 g/1½ lb gooseberries, topped and tailed
2 tablespoons water
50 g/2 oz sugar, to taste
2 teaspoons egg replacer mixed with
2 tablespoons water
300 ml/½ pint milk substitute
finely grated rind of 1 lemon
mint or lavender sprigs, to decorate

1 Put the gooseberries into a saucepan with the water and half the sugar. Bring to the boil and simmer for about 15 minutes until the gooseberries are soft. Lift out the fruit with a slotted spoon and place in a food processor or blender, leaving the juice in the pan.

2 Blend the gooseberries to a smooth purée, adding the rest of the sugar if necessary. Boil the juice to reduce to 175 ml/6 fl oz. Cool slightly and stir in the egg replacer mixture. Simmer for 2–3 minutes, beating constantly.

3 Fold in the gooseberry purée, the milk substitute and grated lemon rind.

4 Pour into a shallow freezer container and freeze for 45 minutes, then tip the ice cream into a food processor or blender and process for 30–60 seconds. Put the ice cream back in the freezer. Repeat the puréeing and freezing processes twice, then freeze the ice cream until firm. Serve scooped into glass bowls and topped with mint or lavender sprigs.

Exotic pineapple sorbet

Serves 6
Preparation: 20 minutes, plus cooling and freezing
Cooking: 5 minutes

Nutritional Information

Per serving:
Energy 79 kcals/339 kJ
Protein 1 g
Carbohydrate 20 g
Fat 0 g
Fibre 2 g
Calcium 28 mg
Iron 0 mg

flesh of 1 large pineapple

2 teaspoons vegetarian gelling agent (optional)

300 ml/½ pint unsweetened mango or pineapple juice

100 ml/3½ fl oz water

2 teaspoons egg replacer, mixed with 4 tablespoons water

1 Purée the pineapple flesh in a food processor or blender until smooth. Tip it into a bowl.

2 Mix the gelling agent to a smooth paste with a little of the mango or pineapple juice, then stir it back into the remaining mango or pineapple juice. Pour into a saucepan and add the water. Bring to the boil and boil for 2 minutes. Leave to cool, then add to the pineapple purée.

3 Pour the mixture into a shallow freezer container and freeze for 2 hours, or until almost set. Place in a food processor or blender and reduce to a mush.

4 Whisk the egg replacer and water mixture until stiff, then fold it into the half-frozen sorbet. Pour back into the freezer container and freeze until solid. For a very smooth sorbet, purée twice more during the freezing.

TIP:

The gelling agent keeps the sorbet smooth, but can be left out if the sorbet is to be eaten within 24 hours of making.

Fruit-filled pancakes

Makes 8–12 pancakes
Preparation: 10–15 minutes
Cooking: 10 minutes, plus cooking the pancakes

Nutritional Information

Per serving:
Energy 325 kcals / 1364 kJ
Protein 3 g
Carbohydrate 43 g
Fat 17 g
Fibre 4 g
Calcium 20 mg
Iron 1 mg

PANCAKE BATTER:

50 g/2 oz potato flour

50 g/2 oz brown rice flour

2 teaspoons egg replacer

300 ml/½ pint water or milk substitute

sunflower oil, for frying

FILLING:

4 ripe peaches, skinned, stoned and sliced

1 teaspoon mixed spice

50 g/2 oz dairy-free margarine

50 g/2 oz raw cane sugar

1 teaspoon grated orange rind

1 teaspoon grated lemon rind

2 tablespoons orange juice

1 tablespoon lemon juice

1 To make the pancake batter, put the flours, egg replacer and water or milk substitute into a food processor or blender and process for 1 minute until thoroughly mixed.

2 Heat a little oil in a small nonstick frying pan. Pour sufficient batter into the pan just to cover the base. Cook for 1–2 minutes, then turn or toss the pancake and cook the second side. Remove the pancake from the pan and keep warm while making the rest of the pancakes.

3 To make the filling, put the sliced peaches into a bowl and sprinkle the mixed spice over them. Heat the margarine with the sugar in a frying pan and add the spiced peach slices. Turn them to coat, then add the orange and lemon rinds and juice and simmer for a few minutes.

4 Fill the hot pancakes with the peach mixture and fold into quarters. Serve with the pan juices.

Totally tropical fruit salad

Serves 4
Preparation: 20 minutes, plus chilling

Nutritional Information

Per serving:
Energy 119 kcals/506 kJ
Protein 2 g
Carbohydrate 28 g
Fat 1 g
Fibre 3 g
Calcium 39 mg
Iron 1 mg

Refreshing fruit salad

1 mango, peeled, stoned
and sliced
2 apples, cored and sliced
2 pears, peeled, cored
and chopped
125 g/4 oz seedless grapes
2 passion fruit, halved
and deseeded
125 g/4 oz watermelon,
peeled, deseeded and cubed
¼ teaspoon orange
flower water
150 ml/¼ pint apple juice
mint leaves, to decorate

Serves 6
Preparation: 15 minutes

1 Mix all the fruit together in a
bowl. Combine the orange
flower water with the apple
juice and pour over the fruit.
2 Scatter the fruit salad with
mint leaves and serve on its
own, or with Power muesli (see
page 42), Berry and rice muesli
(see page 40) or yogurt.

1 small pineapple
2 passion fruit
2 kiwifruit, peeled
and quartered
1 mango, peeled, stoned
and sliced
1 ogen or honeydew melon
1 dragon fruit or pitihayas,
peeled and sliced
3 tablespoons mango or
apple juice
2 teaspoons orange
flower water
Creamy topping (see page 81),
to serve

1 Cut the top off the pineapple and remove the skin. Roughly
chop the pineapple flesh, discarding the core. Place the flesh in a
large bowl.
2 Halve the passion fruit and spoon out the flesh, juice and seeds
and mix with the kiwifruit and mango. Add to the pineapple.
3 Cut the melon in half, scoop out the seeds and roughly chop the
flesh and add to the fruit salad together with the dragon fruit or
pitihayas, and mango or apple juice.
4 Sprinkle with orange flower water and chill in the refrigerator
until ready to serve. Serve with creamy topping.

VARIATIONS:

Add any fresh seasonal fruit that your diet allows, such as peaches,
cherries, blackberries, strawberries, kiwifuit, apricots and plums.

Rice & rye bread

Makes one 500 g/1 lb loaf
Preparation: 20 minutes, plus rising
Cooking: 40–50 minutes

Nutritional Information

Per slice:
Energy 175 kcals/745 kJ
Protein 4 g
Carbohydrate 33 g
Fat 3 g
Fibre 1 g
Calcium 9 mg
Iron 1 mg

300 ml/½ pint tepid water

1 teaspoon sugar

15 g/½ oz dried yeast

175 g/6 oz brown rice flour

175 g/6 oz rye flour

1 teaspoon salt

25 ml/1 fl oz sunflower oil

dairy-free margarine, for greasing

1 tablespoon coriander seeds (optional)

½ tablespoon cumin seeds (optional)

1 Put the water in a small jug and stir in the sugar until it dissolves. Sprinkle the yeast on the top and leave in a warm place until it begins to froth.

2 Sift the flours and salt into a large bowl, then add the oil and the yeast mixture. Beat to a thick pouring consistency.

3 Put the bread mixture into a greased 500 g/1 lb loaf tin and seal inside a large polythene bag. Leave the dough to rise in a warm place for about 1 hour or until it has doubled in size. Sprinkle the top of the uncooked dough with the coriander and cumin seeds, if using.

4 Bake the bread in a preheated oven, 200°C (400°F), Gas Mark 6, for 25–30 minutes. Remove the partially baked bread from the tin and place on a baking sheet. Bake for a further 15–20 minutes to make a nice crust.

Soda bread

Makes one 500 g/1lb loaf
Preparation: 10 minutes
Cooking: 40–45 minutes

50 g/2 oz soya flour

300 g/10 oz brown rice flour

½ teaspoon salt

¾ teaspoon cream of tartar

¾ teaspoon bicarbonate of soda

1 tablespoon sunflower oil

275 ml/9 fl oz milk substitute

dairy-free margarine, for greasing

Nutritional Information

Per slice:
Energy 183 kcals/780 kJ
Protein 6 g
Carbohydrate 30 g
Fat 5 g
Fibre 1 g
Calcium 18 mg
Iron 1 mg

1 Put the flours, salt, cream of tartar and bicarbonate of soda in a large bowl. Mix the oil with the milk substitute and combine with the dry ingredients to form a soft dough.

2 Form into a round shape and place on a greased baking sheet. Bake in a preheated oven, 200°C (400°F), Gas Mark 6, for 40–45 minutes.

Fruit soda bread

Add 2–3 tablespoons raisins or sultanas to the dry ingredients.

Soya & rice bread

Makes one 500 g/1 lb loaf
Preparation: 20 minutes, plus rising
Cooking: 30–45 minutes

Nutritional Information

Per slice:
Energy 170 kcals/735 kJ
Protein 6 g
Carbohydrate 30 g
Fat 3 g
Fibre 2 g
Calcium 15 mg
Iron 1 mg

15 g/1½ oz dried yeast

2 teaspoons clear honey

225 ml/7½ fl oz tepid water

300 g/10 oz brown rice flour

50 g/2 oz soya flour

½ teaspoon salt

1 teaspoon egg replacer mixed with

2 tablespoons water

dairy-free margarine, for greasing

1 Mix together the yeast, honey and water in a small jug and leave to froth in a warm place.

2 Sift the rice flour, soya flour and salt into a bowl. Make a well in the centre and add the egg replacer mixture. Add the yeast mixture. Stir to make a smooth stiff batter, adding extra water as needed.

3 Put the bread mixture into a greased 500 g/1 lb loaf tin and seal inside a large polythene bag; leave to rise in a warm place for about 1 hour or until doubled in size. Bake in the centre of a preheated oven, 200°C (400°F), Gas Mark 6, for 30–45 minutes.

VARIATION:

If you like, add 2 rosemary sprigs and 1 tablespoon pumpkin seeds to the top of the uncooked dough before baking.

Tortillas & flatbreads

Makes 8 tortillas
Preparation: 10–15 minutes, plus standing
Cooking: 2 ½ minutes per tortilla

Nutritional Information

Per serving:
Energy 69 kcals/289 kJ
Protein 2 g
Carbohydrate 14 g
Fat 1 g
Fibre 0 g
Calcium 4 mg
Iron 1 mg

150 g/5 oz cornmeal (maize flour)
pinch of salt
pinch of chilli powder (optional)
about 175 ml/6 fl oz tepid water

1 Place the cornmeal, salt and chilli, if using, in a bowl. Add the water gradually, kneading to form a smooth soft dough. Divide into 8 pieces, cover and leave to stand for 1 hour.

2 Place each piece of dough between 2 sheets of clingfilm and roll into rounds 13 cm/5 inches in diameter.

3 Heat an ungreased heavy frying pan. When hot, place a tortilla in the pan. Cook for about 1 minute or until golden speckles appear on the surface. Turn the tortilla and cook the other side for 1–1½ minutes.

4 Wrap in a warm cloth and keep hot while cooking the remainder.

Tortilla chips

Cut each uncooked tortilla into 6 equal triangles and deep-fry in corn oil at 180°C (350°F), Gas Mark 4, until golden and crisp. Do not overcook. Drain on kitchen paper.

Spicy cornmeal flatbread

Add 1 teaspoon Wheat-free baking powder (see page 96) and 1 teaspoon ground cumin, cumin seeds, caraway or onion seeds to the cornmeal before mixing with the water. Make the dough straight away into thicker cakes. Cook in a frying pan with a little oil (1 tablespoon per tortilla) until golden brown on both sides. Dry on kitchen paper. Serve hot or cold.

Fruit malt loaf

Makes one 500 g/1lb loaf
Preparation: 15–20 minutes, plus rising
Cooking: 45 minutes

Nutritional Information

Per slice:
Energy 230 kcals/980 kJ
Protein 5 g
Carbohydrate 42 g
Fat 6 g
Fibre 2 g
Calcium 49 mg
Iron 2 mg

25 g/½ oz easy-blend dried yeast

150 ml/¼ pint tepid water

1 teaspoon clear honey

125 g/4 oz brown rice flour

125 g/4 oz rye flour

125 g/4 oz sultanas or raisins

50 g/2 oz dairy-free margarine, plus
extra for greasing

100 g/4 oz malt extract

50 g/2 oz black treacle or molasses

1 tablespoon clear honey, to glaze

fruit purée, to serve

1 Mix together the yeast, water and honey and leave to froth in a warm place.
2 Mix the flours, yeast mixture and sultanas or raisins in a warm bowl. Put the margarine, malt extract and black treacle or molasses into a saucepan and heat gently until the margarine has melted. Leave to cool.
3 Add the treacle mixture to the dry ingredients and mix to a soft dough. Transfer to a greased 500 g/1 lb loaf tin, cover with a damp cloth and leave in a warm place for about 1 hour or until doubled in sauce.
4 Bake in the centre of a preheated oven, 200°C (400°F), Gas Mark 6, for 45 minutes. Turn out on to a wire rack, brush with honey, then leave to cool. Serve in thick slices and spread with fruit purée.

Fruit cake

Makes one 23 cm/9 inch cake
Preparation: 20–30 minutes
Cooking: 1 hour

Nutritional Information

Per slice:
Energy 420 kcals/1789 kJ
Protein 8 g
Carbohydrate 85 g
Fat 7 g
Fibre 8 g
Calcium 73 mg
Iron 3 mg

Wheat-free baking powder:

125 g/4 oz rice flour
50 g/2 oz bicarbonate of soda
50 g/2 oz tartaric acid

Preparation: 5–10 minutes

1 Mix together all the ingredients and sieve several times. Store the powder in a screw-top jar.

300 ml/½ pint tepid pineapple juice
15 g/½ oz dried yeast
50 g/2 oz soya flour
50 g/2 oz millet flour
250 g/8 oz brown rice flour
1 tablespoon Wheat-free baking powder (see box)
2 teaspoons ground cinnamon
2 tablespoons sunflower oil
500 g/1 lb mixture of prunes, sultanas, raisins and currants
125 g/4 oz chopped dates
2 cooking apples, peeled and chopped

1 Put the pineapple juice into a small jug and sprinkle the yeast on the top. Leave to froth.
2 Put the soya flour, millet flour, brown rice flour, baking powder and cinnamon into a bowl. Stir in the oil.
3 Put the dried fruit mixture into a food processor or blender and chop. Add the dried fruit mixture and the frothy pineapple juice mixture to the flours and stir well so it has a sloppy consistency, adding more juice if needed.
4 Spoon the mixture into a greased 23 cm/9 inch cake tin and bake in a preheated oven, 180°C (350°F), Gas Mark 4, for about 1 hour. Leave to cool for a few minutes in the tin, then transfer to a wire rack to cool completely.

Berry fruit scones

Makes 15 scones
Preparation: 10–15 minutes
Cooking: 15–20 minutes

50 g/2 oz buckwheat flour

150 g/5 oz brown rice flour

2 teaspoons Wheat-free baking powder (see page 96)

50 g/2 oz dairy-free margarine or goats' butter, plus extra for greasing

50 g/2 oz dried cranberries, blueberries, sour cherries or sultanas

125 g/4 oz grated apple, with skin

about 8 tablespoons milk substitute

Nutritional Information

Per serving:
Energy 88 kcals/370 kJ
Protein 1 g
Carbohydrate 14 g
Fat 3 g
Fibre 1 g
Calcium 10 mg
Iron 0 mg

1 Sift together the flours and baking powder and rub in the margarine or butter. Add the dried fruit and grated apple and mix to a soft dough with the milk substitute.

2 Drop spoonfuls of the mixture on to a greased baking sheet. Bake in a preheated oven, 230°C (450°F), Gas Mark 8, for 15–20 minutes until light golden brown. Cool on a wire rack.

TIP:

Serve these scones with goat's butter or yogurt and fruit purées.

Crumble jam squares

Makes 24 squares
Preparation: 10 minutes
Cooking: 30 minutes

Nutritional Information

Per serving:
Energy 170 kcals/712 kJ
Protein 1 g
Carbohydrate 21 g
Fat 9 g
Fibre 1 g
Calcium 10 mg
Iron 1 mg

175 g/6 oz rolled oats

175 g/6 oz brown rice flour

250 g/8 oz dairy-free margarine or goats' butter, plus extra for greasing

125 g/4 oz raw cane soft light brown sugar

50 g/2 oz dried fruit, chopped

1 teaspoon cinnamon

½ teaspoon bicarbonate of soda

5 tablespoons additive-free cherry jam

1 Place all the ingredients except the jam in a large bowl and beat the mixture until it is crumbly. Reserve 3–4 tablespoons of the mixture, then press the rest into a well greased 32 x 23 cm/13 x 9 inch baking tray. Spread evenly with jam and sprinkle with the reserved mixture.

2 Bake in a preheated oven, 200°C (400°F), Gas Mark 6, for 30 minutes until golden. Leave the cake to cool in the tin then cut into squares.

Choc-chip brownies

Makes 16 brownies
Preparation: 15 minutes
Cooking: 35 minutes

Nutritional Information

Per serving:
Energy 100 kcals/427 kJ
Protein 1 g
Carbohydrate 13 g
Fat 6 g
Fibre 1 g
Calcium 8 mg
Iron 0 mg

50 g/2 oz dairy-free margarine

125 g/4 oz raw cane soft dark brown sugar

1 teaspoon egg replacer mixed with

2 tablespoons water

¼ teaspoon natural vanilla extract

50 g/2 oz brown rice flour

1 teaspoon Wheat-free baking powder (see page 96)

50 g/2 oz desiccated coconut

50 g/2 oz bitter chocolate (70% cocoa solids) chopped

1 Line the base of a shallow 17.5 cm/7 inch square tin with silicone paper. Melt the margarine in a saucepan over a gentle heat, then mix in the sugar and stir until dissolved.

2 Cool slightly and beat in the egg replacer mixture and vanilla extract.

3 Sift together the flour and baking powder and mix in thoroughly. Stir in the coconut and chopped chocolate and pour into the prepared tin. Bake in a preheated oven, 190°C (375°F), Gas Mark 5, for about 30 minutes or until set, but not hard.

4 Cut the cake mixture into 16 squares while still hot, then leave to cool in the tin. When cold, lift out carefully and store in an airtight container until required.

Pineapple & carrot cake

Makes one 20 cm/8 inch cake
Preparation: 15–20 minutes
Cooking: 1 hour

Nutritional Information

Per slice:
Energy 233 kcals/980 kJ
Protein 2 g
Carbohydrate 34 g
Fat 11 g
Fibre 1 g
Calcium 98 mg
Iron 1 mg

125 g/4 oz dairy-free margarine or
goat's butter, plus extra for greasing
125 g/4 oz golden caster sugar
1 teaspoon ground cinnamon
2 teaspoons egg replacer mixed with
4 tablespoons water
75 g/3 oz raw carrot, finely grated
75 g/3 oz pineapple, finely chopped
1–2 tablespoons pineapple juice
250 g/8 oz self-raising flour
icing sugar or Lemon creamy topping (see
page 81), to decorate

1 Cream the margarine or butter and sugar in a bowl until pale and fluffy. Beat in the ground cinnamon. Gradually add the egg replacer mixture, beating well after each addition.

2 Stir in the grated carrot, chopped pineapple and pineapple juice. Sift the flour into the bowl and fold into the creamed mixture.

3 Spoon the mixture into a greased 20 cm/8 inch cake tin and bake in a preheated oven, 180°C (350°F), Gas Mark 4, for 1 hour or until a warm skewer inserted in the centre of the cake comes out clean. Leave the cake to cool in the tin. Turn out and dust liberally with sifted icing sugar or spread with lemon creamy topping.

TIP:
The flavour of this cake improves if it is kept for a day before eating.

Apple & spice cake

Makes one 20 cm/8 inch cake
Preparation: 15 minutes
Cooking: 1¼-½ hours

Nutritional Information

Per slice:
Energy 287 kcals/1211 kJ
Protein 3 g
Carbohydrate 47 g
Fat 11 g
Fibre 4 g
Calcium 29 mg
Iron 1 mg

125 g/4 oz potato flour

125 g/4 oz brown rice flour

½ teaspoon ground cinnamon

½ teaspoon mixed spice (optional)

½ teaspoon bicarbonate of soda

125 g/4 oz dairy-free margarine or goats' butter, plus extra for greasing

125 g/4 oz currants

175 g/6 oz sultanas

250 g/8 oz cooking apples, peeled, cored and coarsely grated

2 teaspoons egg replacer mixed with 4 tablespoons water

1 Granny Smith apple, peeled, cored and thinly sliced

2 tablespoons apricot conserve, sieved and warmed

1 Sift together the flours, cinnamon, mixed spice, if using, and bicarbonate of soda. Rub the margarine or butter into the flour until it resembles fine breadcrumbs. Mix in the currants, sultanas and grated apple and bind with the egg replacer mixture.

2 Turn into a greased and lined 20 cm/8 inch round cake tin, level the top and arrange the Granny Smith apple slices over the top of the mixture. Bake in a preheated oven, 180°C (350°)F, Gas Mark 4, for 1¼–1½ hours or until the cake is firm to the touch and a warm skewer inserted in the centre comes out clean.

3 Turn out the cake and cool on a wire rack. Once cooled, brush the cake with the apricot glaze.

Chocolate & buckwheat cake

Makes one 15 cm/6 inch cake
Preparation: 20–30 minutes, plus cooling
Cooking: 40 minutes

Nutritional Information

Per slice:
Energy 464 kcals/1936 kJ
Protein 6 g
Carbohydrate 53 g
Fat 27 g
Fibre 0 g
Calcium 56 mg
Iron 1 mg

175 g/6 oz buckwheat flour

40 g/1½ oz carob powder

1½ teaspoons Wheat-free
baking powder (see page 96)

175 g/6 oz raw cane soft dark
brown sugar

175 g/6 oz dairy-free
margarine or goats' butter,
plus extra for greasing

1½ tablespoons water

3 eggs

FILLING:

2 tablespoons powdered
soya milk

1 tablespoon cold water

3 tablespoons clear honey

25 g/1 oz carob or bitter
chocolate (70% cocoa solids)

50 g/2 oz dairy-free margarine
or goats' butter

icing sugar, to decorate

1 Sift the flour, carob and baking powder into a large mixing bowl. Add the sugar, margarine and water and beat thoroughly for 1 minute. Add the eggs and continue beating for 1 minute, occasionally scraping the mixture away from the sides of the bowl.

2 Divide the mixture between two greased and lined 15cm/6 inch sandwich tins and smooth the tops. Bake in a preheated oven, 180°C (350°F), Gas Mark 4, for 35 minutes or until a warm skewer inserted into the centre comes out clean. Leave to cool in the tins for a few minutes, then turn the cakes out on to a wire rack to cool completely.

3 To make the filling, mix the powdered soya milk and water into a paste, then put it into a heavy-based saucepan with the honey, carob or bitter chocolate, and margarine or goat's butter. Heat gently, stirring until the mixture is smooth. Remove the pan from the heat and leave the mixture to cool completely and thicken, then use it to sandwich the cakes together.

4 Sprinkle the top of the cake with sifted icing sugar.

Gluten-free sponge cake

Makes one 15 cm/6 inch cake
Preparation: 10–15 minutes, plus cooling
Cooking: 12–15 minutes

Nutritional Information

Per serving:
Energy 403 kcals/1687 kJ
Protein 3 g
Carbohydrate 44 g
Fat 25 g
Fibre 1 g
Calcium 23 mg
Iron 0 mg

Freezer jam

1.2 litres/2 pints allowed fruit, puréed
1 tablespoon arrowroot
sugar, to taste (optional)

Preparation: 5–10 minutes
Cooking: about 5 minutes

1 Put the fruit purée into a saucepan. Combine a little of the purée with the arrowroot to form a smooth paste, then return to the purée in the pan and stir in.
2 Add sugar to taste, if liked, and heat the mixture. Cook for 3–4 minutes. If it is too thick, thin with fruit juice. Leave to cool.
3 Put the jam into small rigid containers. It can be frozen for up to 3 months. Once thawed, the jam with keep for 7 days in the refrigerator.

175 g/6 oz dairy-free margarine or goats' butter, plus extra for greasing
75 g/3 oz golden caster sugar
3 teaspoons egg replacer mixed with 6 tablespoons water
175 g/6 oz brown rice flour
40 g/1½ oz buckwheat flour
1½ teaspoons Wheat-free baking powder (see page 96)
3 tablespoons additive-free or Freezer jam (see box)
icing sugar, to decorate

1 Cream the margarine or butter and sugar until soft and fluffy. Gradually add the egg replacer mixture, beating well. Lightly mix in the flours and baking powder, adding a little extra tepid water if the mixture seems stiff.
2 Divide the cake mixture between two 15 cm/6 inch greased sponge tins. Bake in a preheated oven, 200°C (400°F), Gas Mark 6, for 12–15 minutes or until the cakes spring back when lightly pressed.
3 Turn out the cakes on to a wire rack to cool.
4 Spread one sponge with jam and place the other one on top. Dust with sifted icing sugar.

Millet & rice savoury biscuits

Makes 20 biscuits
Preparation: 10 minutes
Cooking: 10–15 minutes

125 g/4 oz millet flour

125 g/4 oz brown rice flour

¼ teaspoon salt

2 teaspoons Wheat-free baking powder (see page 96)

50 g/2 oz dairy-free margarine or goats' butter, plus extra for greasing

100 ml/3½ fl oz water

Nutritional Information

Per serving:
Energy 84 kcals/355 kJ
Protein 1 g
Carbohydrate 13 g
Fat 3 g
Fibre 0 g
Calcium 3 mg
Iron 0 mg

1 Combine the flours, salt and baking powder in a bowl. Rub in the margarine or butter and add the water to make a soft dough.

2 Knead the dough lightly and roll out to 1 cm/½ inch thick. Cut into small rounds, arrange them on a greased baking sheet and bake in a preheated oven, 190°C (375°F), Gas Mark 5, for 10–15 minutes.

3 Leave the biscuits to cool on the baking sheet, then transfer to an airtight container until required.

TIP:

To make delicious party canapés, spread these biscuits with tomato, spinach and carrot purées.

Millet & cranberry flapjacks

Makes 16 flapjacks
Preparation: 10 minutes
Cooking: 30 minutes

125 g/4 oz dairy-free margarine or
goats' butter, plus extra for greasing
50 g/2 oz unrefined demerara or raw
cane light brown sugar
2 tablespoons golden syrup
250 g/8 oz millet flakes or rolled oats
1 tablespoon dried cranberries

Nutritional Information

Per serving:
Energy 147 kcals/615 kJ
Protein 2 g
Carbohydrate 18 g
Fat 8 g
Fibre 1 g
Calcium 13 mg
Iron 1 mg

1 Put the margarine or butter, sugar and syrup into a saucepan and gently heat until the fat and sugar have melted. Remove the pan from the heat and add the millet flakes or rolled oats and dried cranberries, mixing thoroughly.

2 Grease a 20 cm/8 inch square sandwich tin. Spoon the flapjack mixture into the prepared tin and spread flat with a palette knife. Bake in a preheated oven, 180°C (350°F), Gas Mark 4, for about 30 minutes or until golden brown.

3 Leave the flapjacks to cool in the tin for about 5 minutes, mark into 16 portions. Leave to cool completely, then remove the flapjacks from the tin and store in an airtight container until required.

Spice biscuits

Makes 15 biscuits
Preparation: 15 minutes
Cooking: 15–20 minutes

125 g/4 oz dairy-free margarine or
goats' butter, plus extra for greasing
50 g/2 oz raw cane soft dark
brown sugar
50 g/2 oz mashed cooked parsnip
or potato
175 g/6 oz brown rice flour
50 g/2 oz sultanas
1 teaspoon mixed spice

Nutritional Information

Per serving:
Energy 127 kcals/530 kJ
Protein 1 g
Carbohydrate 15 g
Fat 7 g
Fibre 1 g
Calcium 6 mg
Iron 0 mg

1 Cream the dairy-free margarine or butter and sugar until smooth and fluffy, then beat in the parsnip or potato.

2 Add the flour, sultanas and mixed spice and mix well. Turn on to a lightly floured surface and roll out to 5 mm/¼ inch thick. Using a 6 cm/2½ inch cutter, cut out rounds and place them on greased baking sheets.

3 Bake the biscuits in a preheated oven, 180°C (350°F), Gas Mark 4, for 15–20 minutes until golden brown. Leave to cool on the baking sheets, then keep in an airtight container until required.

Fresh coconut cookies

Makes 24 cookies
Preparation: 10 minutes
Cooking: 15–20 minutes

125 g/4 oz dairy-free margarine or
goats' butter, plus extra for greasing
50 g/2 oz golden syrup
50 g/2 oz unrefined demerara sugar
1 teaspoon bicarbonate of soda
50 g/2 oz freshly grated or
desiccated coconut
75 g/3 oz millet flakes
125 g/4 oz brown rice flour

Nutritional Information

Per serving:
Energy 133 kcals/554 kJ
Protein 1 g
Carbohydrate 10 g
Fat 10 g
Fibre 1 g
Calcium 4 mg
Iron 0 mg

1 Put the margarine or butter, golden syrup and sugar into a large saucepan. Stir over a low heat until the fat and sugar have melted. Remove the pan from the heat, add the bicarbonate of soda and stir well to dissolve. (The mixture may rise slightly in the pan during this stage). Add the coconut, millet flakes and flour and blend thoroughly.

2 Cool slightly, then gather the mixture together and roll into about 24 balls.

3 Put the balls on 2 greased baking sheets, allowing plenty of space for the mixture to spread out during cooking. Gently press the balls flat.

4 Bake the cookies in a preheated oven, 160°C (325°F), Gas Mark 3, for 15–20 minutes or until golden brown. Leave them on the baking sheets until almost cold, then transfer to wire racks to cool completely.

Gluten-free lemon shortbread

Makes 8 pieces
Preparation: 10 minutes, plus chilling
Cooking: 35–40 minutes

Nutritional Information

Per serving:
Energy 224 kcals/940 kJ
Protein 2 g
Carbohydrate 25 g
Fat 13 g
Fibre 0 g
Calcium 6 mg
Iron 0 mg

150 g/5 oz brown rice flour
25 g/1 oz ground rice
finely grated rind of 1 lemon
50 g/2 oz golden caster sugar
125 g/4 oz dairy-free margarine or
goats' butter, plus extra for greasing
1 tablespoon unrefined
demerara sugar

1 Sift the flour and ground rice into a bowl and stir in the grated lemon rind and sugar. Add the margarine or butter and rub in, then knead lightly to make a smooth dough. Do not overwork the dough or it will become sticky. Cover and chill the dough for 30 minutes.

2 Press the dough into an 18 cm/7 inch plain round or fluted flan ring on a greased baking sheet. Prick all over with a fork, then mark the shortbread into wedges. Chill for 15 minutes.

3 Bake the shortbread in a preheated oven, 160°C (325°F), Gas Mark 3, for 35–40 minutes or until pale golden. Remove from the oven and sprinkle with the demerara sugar. Leave to cool slightly on the baking sheet, then transfer to a wire rack to cool completely.

VARIATION:

Use 50 g/2 oz raisins in place of 25 g/1 oz of the sugar.

Owl cookies

Makes 10 cookies
Preparation: 15–20 minutes, plus chilling
Cooking: 8–10 minutes

175 g/6 oz rice flour

1 teaspoon Wheat-free baking powder (see page 96)

75 g/3 oz dairy-free margarine or goats' butter

50 g/2 oz raw cane soft light brown sugar

a few drops of natural vanilla extract

15 g/½ oz cocoa powder

pinch of bicarbonate of soda

raisins

Nutritional Information

Per serving:
Energy 144 kcals/600 kJ
Protein 2 g
Carbohydrate 20 g
Fat 6 g
Fibre 0 g
Calcium 14 mg
Iron 0 mg

1 Sift together the flour and baking powder. Cream the margarine or butter until pale, light and fluffy. Beat in the sugar and the vanilla extract.

2 Mix the cocoa powder with a little water and add the bicarbonate of soda.

3 Add the flour and baking powder to the creamed mixture and stir until evenly blended. Put two thirds of the dough on a board lightly dusted with rice flour. Stir the cocoa mixture into the remaining third.

4 Shape both mixtures into sausages. Chill in the refrigerator for 30 minutes– 1 hour, until the dough is firm enough to roll out.

5 Divide the larger (light-coloured) piece of dough into 2 pieces and roll each one into a rectangle 10 x 12 cm/4 x 5 inches. Divide the cocoa dough into 2 pieces and roll each one into a 12 cm/5 inch sausage. Place the cocoa sausages on the other dough pieces and roll up. Leave both rolls in the refrigerator for a further 1–2 hours to firm.

6 Cut dough into slices about 5 mm/¼ inch thick. To form the owl's head, place 2 circles side by side and press lightly together. Pinch the top corners of each head to form ear tufts. Use raisins for the eyes.

7 Bake the owls in a preheated oven, 180°C (350°F), Gas Mark 4, for 8–10 minutes. Transfer carefully to a wire rack to cool.

Muesli snack crunch

Makes 625 g/1¼lb
Preparation: 15 minutes
Cooking: 35–40 minutes

125 g/4 oz dairy-free margarine or
goats' butter
125 g/4 oz clear honey
25 g/1 oz cornflakes, crushed
175 g/6 oz millet flakes
150 g/5 oz raisins or chopped dates

Nutritional Information

Per serving:
Energy 80 kcals/335 kJ
Protein 1 g
Carbohydrate 12 g
Fat 4 g
Fibre <1 g
Calcium 5 mg
Iron 0 mg

1 Combine the margarine or butter and honey in a large saucepan and cook over a low heat, stirring constantly until the mixture is well blended and smooth. Remove from the heat and stir in the cornflakes and millet. Mix until well coated, then transfer the mixture to an ungreased 30 x 25 cm/12 x 10 inch baking sheet.
2 Bake in a preheated oven, 160°C (325°F), Gas Mark 3, or 35–40 minutes or until golden. Stir occasionally.
3 Remove from the oven, add the raisins or dates and mix well. Transfer to a cold ungreased baking sheet to cool. Store in an airtight container until required.

VARIATIONS:

Add 25 g/1 oz chopped nuts, dried banana, chopped papaya or crystallized ginger, or use 25 g/1 oz puffed rice or rolled oats to the crunch instead of the cornflakes.

Hand-dipped toffee apples

Makes 4 toffee apples
Preparation: 5 minutes
Cooking: 10–15 minutes

4 organic dessert apples, such as Cox's
or Russets

500 g/1 lb unrefined granulated sugar

150 ml/¼ pint water

75 g/3 oz chopped and toasted hazelnuts or
grated coconut (optional)

Nutritional Information

Per serving:
Energy 660 kcals/2800 kJ
Protein 3 g
Carbohydrate 144 g
Fat 12 g
Fibre 4 g
Calcium 33 mg
Iron 1 mg

1 Wash the apples and dry them thoroughly. Push a stick into the core of each apple.

2 Put the sugar and water into a saucepan over a gentle heat and stir frequently. When the sugar has completely dissolved, increase the heat and let the syrup boil rapidly until it turns a golden caramel. Remove from the heat.

3 Quickly swirl each apple in the caramel and place it on a lightly oiled baking sheet. Alternatively, quickly dip them into the chopped toasted hazelnuts or toasted coconut. Leave until set. If the caramel hardens before the apples are coated, return it to the heat to melt.

4 When the caramel has set, wrap the toffee apples in coloured cellophane.

TIPS:

These toffee apples are best eaten on the day they are made when the caramel is hard. Apples with a waxy shine are not suitable for this recipe, because the toffee will not stick to the apple.

Chocolate crunch crisps

Makes 20 crisps
Preparation: 5–10 minutes, plus chilling
Cooking: 5 minutes

125 g/4 oz dairy-free margarine or goats' butter

2 tablespoons golden syrup

25 g/1 oz cocoa powder

250 g/8 oz puffed rice or millet

125 g/4 oz dried cranberries or raisins

Nutritional Information

Per serving:
Energy 120 kcals/507 kJ
Protein 1 g
Carbohydrate 18 g
Fat 6 g
Fibre 1 g
Calcium 1 mg
Iron 1 mg

1 Place the margarine or butter and golden syrup in a large heavy saucepan and heat, stirring, until the margarine melts.

2 Add a little of the syrup mixture to the cocoa powder and mix to form a smooth paste, then return the paste to the saucepan and blend well. Add the puffed rice or millet and cranberries or raisins and stir carefully until evenly coated.

3 Divide between 20 paper sweet cases. Chill the crisps until set.

VARIATIONS:

Use 50 g/2 oz desiccated coconut instead of the cocoa powder. Use corn or millet flakes instead of puffed rice or millet, if preferred.

Fresh apple lollies

Makes 4 lollies
Preparation: 10–15 minutes,
plus cooling and freezing
Cooking: 10–20 minutes

500 g/1 lb cooking apples, peeled, cored
and chopped
clear honey

Nutritional Information

Per serving:
Energy 80 kcals/340 kJ
Protein 0 g
Carbohydrate 21 g
Fat 0 g
Fibre 3 g
Calcium 6 mg
Iron 0 mg

1 Put the apples into a saucepan and add just enough water to cover the bottom of the pan. Simmer gently for 10–20 minutes until very tender.
2 Purée the apples in a food processor or blender or press through a sieve to make a very smooth purée. Sweeten to taste with honey.
3 Leave the purée to cool, then pour it into lolly moulds or ice cube trays and freeze until mushy. Add sticks and continue freezing until set.

VARIATIONS:

Other fruit purées can be used instead of the apples: gently simmer apricots, plums, peaches or blackcurrants. Other fruits, such as raspberries, strawberries, blueberries, kiwifruits and melons, can be blended uncooked with unsweetened apple juice and frozen.

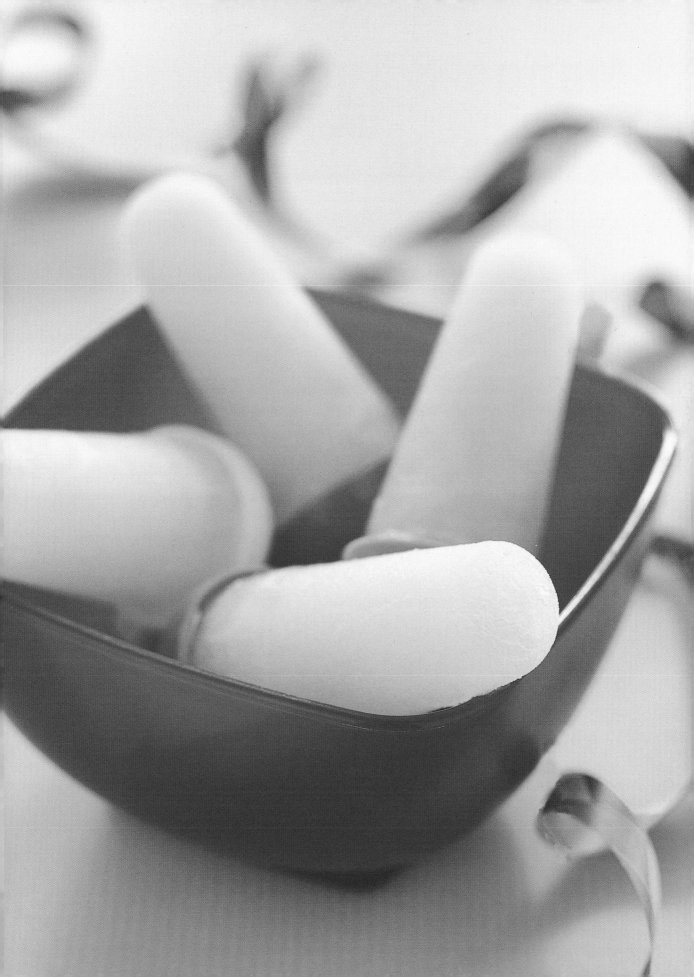

Mango & lychee ice cream

Preparation : 10 minutes, plus freezing

1 large mango, peeled, stoned and roughly chopped
600 ml/1 pint milk
400 g/13 oz can lychees, drained and roughly chopped
1 tablespoon clear honey, to taste
3–4 tablespoons corn oil

Nutritional Information

Per serving:
Energy 190 kcals/800 kJ
Protein 4 g
Carbohydrate 22 g
Fat 10 g
Fibre 1 g
Calcium 120 mg
Iron 1 mg

1 Put the mango flesh into a food processor or blender and purée until smooth.
2 Turn into a bowl and add the milk, lychees, honey and corn oil. Combine the ingredients well, then freeze in an ice-cream maker. Alternatively, put the mixture in the freezer until it begins to set, then process in a food processor or blender.
3 Return to the bowln and place in the freezer and repeat the process twice more for a smooth ice cream.

Carob ice cream

Omit the mango and lychees and add 2 tablespoons carob powder to the mixture before freezing.

Tick-tock birthday cake

Makes one 20 cm/8 inch cake
Preparation: 30–40 minutes
Cooking: 1 hour

Nutritional Information

Per serving:
Energy 540 kcals/2279 kJ
Protein 6 g
Carbohydrate 94 g
Fat 18 g
Fibre 3 g
Calcium 64 mg
Iron 2 mg

125 g/4 oz dairy-free margarine or goats' butter, plus extra for greasing
125 g/4 oz golden caster sugar
1 teaspoon ground cinnamon
2 teaspoons egg replacer mixed with 4 tablespoons water
75 g/3 oz finely grated carrot
125 g/4 oz pineapple, finely chopped
2 tablespoons pineapple juice
125 g/4 oz potato flour
50 g/2 oz brown rice flour
50 g/2 oz soya flour
2 teaspoons Wheat-free baking powder (see page 96)

CAROB FUDGE ICING:

50 g/2 oz dairy-free margarine or goats' butter
3 tablespoons milk substitute
250 g/8 oz icing sugar, sifted
1 tablespoon carob or cocoa powder, sifted

GLACE ICING:

50 g/2 oz icing sugar, sifted
about 1½ teaspoons warm water

1 Cream the margarine or butter and sugar in a large bowl until pale and fluffy. Beat in the cinnamon, if using. Gradually add the egg replacer mixture, beating well after each addition. Stir in the carrot, pineapple and pineapple juice.

2 Sift together the flours and baking powder and fold into the creamed mixture.

3 Spoon the cake mixture into a greased and lined 20 cm/8 inch round cake tin and bake in a preheated oven, 180°C (350°F), Gas Mark 4, for 1 hour. Turn on to a wire rack to cool. The flavour of the cake improves if it is kept for one day before eating.

4 To make the carob fudge icing, melt the margarine or butter in a small saucepan with the milk substitute. Add the icing sugar and carob or cocoa powder and beat well until smooth and glossy. Leave until lukewarm, then pour over the cake so that it runs down the sides and coats them well.

5 To make the glacé icing, put the icing sugar into a bowl and gradually add the water. The icing sugar and water mixture should be thick enough to coat the back of the spoon thickly. Put the glacé icing into a piping bag fitted with a writing nozzle. Pipe on the clock numbers and the hands pointing to the child's age.

Index

acknowledgements

Executive Editor: Nicola Hill
Editor: Rachel Lawrence
Senior Designer: Joanna Bennett
Designer: Claire Harvey
Production Controller: Louise Hall

Special Photography: William Reavell
Food Stylist: Oona van den Berg

all other photography
Getty Images /Stone 3 top, 3 centre below, 8, 14, 17, /Telegraph 18 bottom, 24.
Octopus Publishing Group Limited/Jean Cazals 19 detail 9, 23 detail 5, /Simon Conroy 19 detail 10, /Jeremy Hopley 27 bottom, /Sandra Lane 22 detail 6, /William Lingwood 4 centre above, 9 top, /David Loftus 22 detail 7, /Neil Mersh 19 detail 7, /Sean Myers 22 detail 5, /Peter Pugh-Cook 7, 27 top, 35, /William Reavell 3 centre above, 4 bottom, 6 bottom, 9 bottom, 9 centre above, 9 centre below, 18 top, 19 detail 1, 19 detail 2, 20, 22 detail 1, 23 detail 1, 23 detail 2, 23 detail 7, 23 detail 8, 26, 28, 29, 30, 31 left, 31 centre right, 31 bottom right, 32, 34, 36 top, 36 bottom, 39, 41, 47, 51, 53, 57, 61, 65, 71, 73, 77, 81, 85, 89, 91, 96, 101, 103, 109, 113, 115, 119, 121, 123, 125, /Gareth Sambridge 10, /Simon Smith 4 top, 4 centre below, 19 detail 11, 22 detail 3, /Ian Wallace 3 bottom right, 6 top, 6 centre, 23 detail 3, 23 detail 4, 33, /Philip Webb 19 detail 5, 23 detail 6.
Photodisc 1 left, 1 right, 1 centre, 19 detail 3, 19 detail 4, 19 detail 6, 19 detail 8, 21, 22 detail 2, 22 detail 4.
Science Photo Library /BSIP EDWIGE 11.